Personal Tax
(Finance Act 2016)

Tutorial

for assessments from January 2017

Aubrey Penning
Bob Thomas

Published by Osborne Books Limited
Tel 01905 748071
Email books@osbornebooks.co.uk
Website www.osbornebooks.co.uk

Design by Laura Ingham

Printed by CPI Group (UK) Limited, Croydon, CR0 4YY, on environmentally friendly, acid-free paper from managed forests.

British Library Cataloguing in Publication Data
A catalogue record for this book is available from the British Library

ISBN 978 1909173 941

Contents

Please note that the seven chapters and subsequent sections of the book each have a self-contained numbering system, rather than the traditional form of pagination which runs through the book.

Also available from Osborne Books...

Workbooks

Practice questions and assessments
with answers

Student Zone

Login to access your free ebooks and
interactive revision crosswords

Download **Osborne Books App** free from the App Store or Google Play Store
to view your ebooks online or offline on your mobile or tablet.

www.osbornebooks.co.uk

Introduction

Qualifications covered

This book has been written specifically to cover the Unit 'Personal Tax' which is an optional Unit for the following qualifications:

AAT Professional Diploma in Accounting – Level 4

AAT Professional Diploma in Accounting at SCQF – Level 8

The book contains a clear text with worked examples and case studies, chapter summaries and key terms to help with revision. Each chapter concludes with a wide range of activities, many in the style of AAT computer based assessments.

Osborne Study and Revision Materials

The materials featured on the previous page are tailored to the needs of students studying this unit and revising for the assessment. They include:

- **Workbooks:** paperback books with practice activities and exams
- **Student Zone:** access to Osborne Books online resources
- **Osborne Books App:** Osborne Books ebooks for mobiles and tablets

Visit www.osbornebooks.co.uk for details of study and revision resources and access to online material.

Exams, Finance Acts and tax years

This book has been designed to include guidance and exercises based on Tax Year 2016/17 (Finance Act 2016). We understand that the AAT plan to assess this legislation from 1 January 2017 to 31 December 2017. Tutors and students are advised to check this with the AAT and ensure that they sit the correct computer based assessment.

Note that the pagination of each chapter is self-contained, eg Chapter 1 contains pages 1.0 to 1.25.

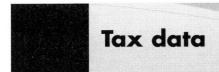

Tax data

INCOME TAX

Personal allowance £11,000
(subject to restrictions)
Personal savings allowance – basic rate taxpayers £1,000
      – higher rate taxpayers £500
Dividend allowance £5,000

Tax rates

	Starting rate	Basic rate	Higher rate	Additional rate
General Income	N/A	20%	40%	45%
Savings Income	0%	20%	40%	45%

		Dividend ordinary rate	Dividend upper rate	Dividend additional rate
Dividend Income		7.5%	32.5%	38.1%

Tax bands £
Starting rate   to 5,000 (Savings Income only)
Basic rate/dividend ordinary rate   to 32,000
Higher rate/dividend upper rate   32,001 – 150,000
Additional rate/dividend additional rate   over 150,000

Company Car Benefit

% of List Price	g/km
7%*	0-50
11%*	51-75
15%*	76-94
16%*	95
17%*	100
18%*	105

. . . and so on to a maximum of 37%
*add 3% for diesel (to a maximum of 37%)

Company Car Fuel Benefit

Percentage for car (see company car benefit on previous page) x £22,200

Authorised Mileage Rates (Mileage Allowance Payments – MAPs)

Cars and vans	First 10,000 miles in tax year	45p per mile
	Additional mileage	25p per mile
Motor cycles		24p per mile
Bicycles		20p per mile

NATIONAL INSURANCE CONTRIBUTIONS (NICS)

Employee's (primary) Class 1 rates:

£155 – £827 per week	12%
above £827 per week	2%

Employer's (secondary) Class 1 rates:

above £156 per week	13.8%

Employer's Class 1A rates:

all taxable benefits in kind	13.8%

CAPITAL GAINS TAX

Annual Exempt Amount

£11,100

CGT rate

Main rates	10% or 20%
Rates on residential property	18% or 28%

1 Introduction to taxation

this chapter covers...

We start this chapter with an overview of the basic principles underlying taxation systems in general. We then go on to examine various tax structures and learn how to distinguish between progressive, proportional and regressive tax systems.

This is followed by a brief examination of the role of HMRC in the UK tax system and how law governs the way that tax is levied.

We then move on to start our study of Income Tax. We see how a basic computation is compiled and how income is divided up for tax purposes. The basis of assessment of the categories of income that we need to understand is also covered here, along with how tax bands work to calculate the total tax. The main forms of exempt income are also noted.

Next we look at the responsibilities of the taxpayer, including an understanding of tax planning, tax avoidance and tax evasion. This includes a summary of HMRC's approach to aggressive tax avoidance and the development of the 'General Anti Abuse Rule'.

The following section deals with the responsibilities of the tax practitioner, including what the AAT Code of Professional Ethics states.

The chapter is concluded with a section on residence and domicile that will help with understanding of the taxation of overseas income and gains.

TAX SYSTEMS

There are various taxes that apply in the UK. In this book we are going to examine Income Tax, Capital Gains Tax and Inheritance Tax. We will also see how National Insurance Contributions (which are also really a form of taxation) impact on employees and employers.

Before we start looking at the specifics of a particular tax we will take a step back so that we can look at the objectives and functions of taxation generally.

principles of taxation

The underlying premise of taxation is that it is the principal mechanism by which the state pays for the services and facilities that it provides for its citizens, and that all taxpayers should pay their fair contribution.

The principles of taxation are the basic concepts that can (or should) guide those who are developing a tax system. There are various principles that writers have proposed over the years.

As early as 1776, Adam Smith set out four principles in 'Wealth of Nations':

- burden proportionate to the ability to pay
- certainty
- convenience
- efficiency of collection

The main ideas in these principles continue to be used today, and will be referred to in the following list of principles which is a combination of various current ideas.

- **Equity**

This is concerned with **fairness**, and links to the above idea of a proportionate tax burden. There are two main ways that equity can be considered.

The first is **horizontal equity** which means that individuals or businesses in the same situation (for example with the same income) should be treated in the same way (for example by having to pay the same amount of tax).

The second consideration is **vertical equity**. This is concerned that taxation is fair at different levels (for example different income levels) in society. In terms of taxes on income this would mean that those with higher income should pay a greater proportion of their income in tax. We will examine the issue of which tax structures achieve this a little later.

■ **Simplicity**

This means that a tax system has rules which are clear and **understandable**. It includes the idea of **transparency** – so that there is no scope for discretion by tax officers about how much tax is due. This ties in with the principle of **certainty** listed above. Certainty can also be linked to the idea that tax rules should **not change retrospectively**. If a transaction has a particular tax implication when it is undertaken, then future tax laws should not change the position for that transaction.

■ **Convenience**

Although most taxpayers would prefer not to pay tax at all, the method of collection must be convenient. For example, paying income tax through PAYE means that it is immediately deducted from the income to which it relates. Tax should not become due too long after the transactions that created the liability.

■ **Stability**

Since decisions are made by organisations and individuals that have implications for many years, it is important that tax rules are stable, and do not change too radically or frequently. This means that taxation should be **predictable**, since that will help with long term planning.

■ **Neutrality**

This idea is concerned that taxation rules should not unduly distort decisions that individuals and business undertake. Neutrality can help prevent unintended consequences of a taxation policy, as it minimises discrimination in favour of or against any particular economic choice. Some writers admit that all taxes result in behaviour changes and distortions, and that the tax system should be used to change behaviour to improve welfare and efficiency. An example of this is the taxation of tobacco products.

■ **Efficiency**

This principle states that costs of collection, administration and ensuring compliance should be minimised. Even at the extreme, these costs should not be greater than the amount of tax revenue generated. There can be a compromise here with the principle of convenience.

■ **Flexibility**

Taxation systems should be able to keep pace with changes in technology and commerce. The impact of digital and global transactions represents a challenge for tax systems. Tax systems must also be able to respond to any future changes, which are difficult to predict. There must be a balance struck between flexibility and stability.

direct and indirect tax

Taxation can be divided into two types. Direct tax (for example income tax) is a tax which is levied on the income or profits of the person or organisation that pays it, rather than on goods or services. Indirect tax is charged on goods or services that consumers can choose whether to purchase. Although indirect tax is collected by intermediaries (for example retailers) it is ultimately borne by consumers. In the UK, value added tax (VAT) is an example of an indirect tax.

tax structures

A tax structure is the combination of the tax base and the tax rates that are applied to the tax base.

The term '**tax base**' refers to the total income or assets that a tax can be applied to. For example, the tax base relating to income tax is the total taxable income of the population that the tax applies to. The tax threshold relating to income tax is the amount of income above which an individual begins to pay tax. This is determined by the personal allowance, as we will see later on. If the tax threshold is increased, then the tax base will be reduced, and if nothing else changes the total amount of tax raised will be reduced.

Tax rates apply to both direct and indirect taxes. The current income tax rates for general income are 20%, 40% and 45%, which apply to bands of taxable income. We will study how this income tax system works through Chapters 1 to 5 of this book.

progressive, proportional and regressive tax systems

These terms broadly describe how the amount of tax that is payable by individuals or organisations depends on their income or profits. This topic is closely related to the idea of equity (or fairness) that we described as a principle of taxation.

A **progressive** income tax system is one in which the lowest paid individuals pay the smallest proportion of their income in tax (or no tax at all), while the highest paid pay the largest proportion of their income in tax. The current UK income tax system is a progressive system. The following figures relate to taxable general income (after deducting the personal allowance). Different rules can apply to savings and dividend income.

	Taxable income	
Basic rate band	£0 to £32,000	Charged at 20%
Higher rate band	£32,001 to £150,000	Charged at 40%
Additional rate band	over £150,000	Charged at 45%

Most individuals are entitled to a personal allowance which means that the first £11,000 of income per year is tax free.

The higher the individual's income, the more tax will be paid, both in total and as a proportion of their income.

For example, an individual with general income of £20,000 will pay no income tax on the first £11,000, and 20% on the rest, equalling (£9,000 x 20%) £1,800. This represents 9% of their total income.

However, an individual with general income of £60,000 will pay income tax of £13,200. This is based on no income tax on the first £11,000, 20% on the next £32,000 and 40% on the rest. The tax of £13,200 represents 22% of their total income.

If a tax is progressive the **proportion** of total income that is paid in tax will rise throughout the range as **income increases**.

A **proportional** tax system applies the same rate of tax across the range. If an income tax system was proportional there would be no personal allowance and only one tax rate. Although those with higher incomes would pay more tax than those with a lower income, the tax as a proportion of income would be identical.

For example if there was an income tax system with a single rate of 30% and no personal allowance, everyone would pay 30% of their income in tax.

An individual with income of £20,000 would pay £6,000 (30% of £20,000), and an individual with income of £60,000 would pay £18,000 (30% of £60,000). The amount of tax would be higher for higher incomes, but the **proportion** of income that is paid in tax would be the **same**.

Such a system would normally be considered unfair in comparison to a progressive tax system.

A **regressive** tax system is one where the proportion of income paid in tax **reduces** as income rises. Although a regressive income tax system would seem unlikely, there are some taxes that are regressive. National Insurance Contributions (NICs) for employees (that we will study later in this book) are regressive at some levels.

Employment earnings between £8,060 and £43,000 per year attract NI contributions of 12% of earnings within that band. Where earnings exceed £43,000 per year, the excess only attracts additional contributions of 2%.

For example an employee earning **£40,000** per year would pay NIC of (£40,000 – £8,060) x 12% = £3,832.80. This equals about 9.6% of earnings.

However an employee earning **£80,000** per year would pay NIC of (£43,000 – £8,060) x 12% = £4,192.80, plus (£80,000 – £43,000) x 2% = £740.00. The NIC totals £4,932.80 which is equal to less than 6.2% of earnings.

Employees with higher earnings than this would pay an even lower percentage of their earnings in NICs.

Some writers describe VAT as a regressive tax system since more VAT as a proportion of income is paid by those with lower incomes. This is because goods and services on which VAT is charged forms a larger part of the income of the less well off. As VAT is only incurred when money is spent, those with higher incomes pay less VAT as a proportion of income, as they tend to save (instead of spend) part of their earnings.

Any tax which is levied at a flat money amount can be considered regressive, since the amount is a lower proportion of the income of high earners. For example, if a UK television licence fee of £145.50 per year is thought of as a tax then its effect is regressive.

HM Revenue & Customs

In the UK, income tax, capital gains tax, inheritance tax and national insurance contributions are all administered by the government department, formed by the amalgamation of the Inland Revenue and HM Customs & Excise. HM Revenue & Customs contains the following three parts:

■ **taxpayer service offices** are the main offices that the taxpayer deals with, and handle much of the basic income tax assessment and collection functions

■ **taxpayer district offices** deal with more complex tax issues

■ **tax enquiry centres** deal with enquiries and provide forms and leaflets to taxpayers

These three functions are located in offices throughout the UK. In smaller centres some functions may be combined into one office, while in larger towns and cities they may be located separately.

the law governing tax

The authority to impose taxes comes from two sources. The first is legislation passed by parliament, known as 'statute law'. You may have heard of the 'Finance Acts'. These are generally published each year and give details of any changes to taxes. These changes will have been proposed by the Chancellor of the Exchequer (usually in 'the budget') and passed by Parliament. In this book we will be using information from the Finance Act 2016, which relates to the tax year 2016/17. We will see exactly what is meant by tax years later in this chapter.

There are also other statute laws that were designed to create frameworks for the way that certain taxes work that continue to be relevant.

The second source of tax law is called 'case law', and arises from decisions taken in court cases. Taxation can be very complicated, and sometimes disagreements between HM Revenue & Customs and taxpayers result in court cases. The final outcome of such cases can then become 'case law' and influence future interpretation of statute law.

Although there is a substantial amount of both statute law and case law that governs the UK tax system, this book will try to keep references to specific law to a minimum. While it will be important to know the rules that apply to certain situations, you will not be required to quote from the legislation.

information available from HM Revenue & Customs

In addition to the tax law outlined above, there are interpretations and explanations of various issues that are published by HM Revenue & Customs. The main ones are as follows:

- extra-statutory concessions are issued by HM Revenue & Customs when they agree to impose a less strict interpretation of the law than would otherwise apply in particular circumstances
- HM Revenue & Customs statements of practice are public announcements of how the HMRC interpret specific rules
- Guides and Help Sheets are issued to help taxpayers complete the necessary return forms and calculate their tax

A large array of publications and forms can be downloaded from the Gov.uk website at www.gov.uk. It also provides data on rates and allowances for a range of tax years. You will find it useful to have a look at what is available on this site when you have an opportunity. It will also mean that you can obtain copies of tax returns to practice on when you reach that part of your personal tax studies.

AN INTRODUCTION TO INCOME TAX

We will now start our study of one of the main taxes that are examined in this book – Income Tax. We briefly referred to the way that it works in our discussion of progressive tax systems.

The best way to start to understand how it works is to look at the 'Income Tax Computation' which will be based on a tax year.
An outline of an income tax computation is as follows:

	£
Income – both earnings and income from savings	X
Less: Personal allowance	(X)
Taxable Income	X
Tax payable on taxable income	X

A very simple income tax computation could be as follows:

	£
Income from earnings	20,000
Less: Personal Allowance	11,000
Taxable income	9,000
Tax payable at 20%	1,800

Later in this chapter we will deal with income tax computations in more detail, but first we will consider some of the issues that might arise in computing income tax.

HOW INCOME IS DIVIDED UP FOR TAX PURPOSES

The income that an individual generates is divided into categories, depending on what sort of income it is and where it comes from. The categories are simply named after the type of income that they include. This is done so that:

- the correct rules on how to work out the income are used (since these vary with the categories), and
- the correct rates of tax are used (since they can also depend on the type of income)

the main categories of income

'Property Income'	Rental income from land and property.
'Trading Income'	Profits of trades and professions (the self-employed and those in partnership).
'Savings & Investment Income'	UK Interest and UK Dividends.
'Employment, pension and Social Security Income'	Income from employment etc. Income tax is deducted from employment income under the system known as Pay-As-You-Earn (PAYE).

This list and descriptions have been simplified to include only the types of income that you need to know about. It does not include, for example, the categories that relate to overseas income.

tax years

For income tax purposes time is divided into 'tax years' (sometimes called 'fiscal years'). Individuals' income and income tax is worked out separately for each tax year. The tax year runs from 6 April in one calendar year to 5 April in the next calendar year. The tax year running from 6/4/16 to 5/4/17 would be described as the tax year 2016/17.

basis of assessment

As mentioned earlier, the income under each category will have different rules that determine how the income is worked out for tax purposes. The most important of these rules is known as the 'basis of assessment', and this simply considers whether the income assessable is the actual income *receivable* (the accruals basis) or the income *received* in the tax year itself. Later in the book we will look in more detail at the rules that govern each type of income. Here is a list of the main assessment rules for each category of income, with some comments about coverage in this book.

Property Income	**Rental income (after deducting allowable expenses), for the tax year, calculated on an *accruals* basis.**
	We will look in more detail at rental income in Chapter 2.
Trading Income	**Profits on an *accruals* basis (after deducting allowable expenses) for the accounting year that ends in the tax year.**
	In this unit we only need to be aware that profits of the self-employed are included in the income tax calculations of individuals. The calculation of the profit for trading income is dealt with in the Business Tax unit.
Savings and Investment Income	**Gross interest *received* in the tax year.** **Amounts of dividends *received* in the tax year.**
	We will look in more detail at interest received and dividends in Chapter 3.
Employment, Pension and Social Security Income	**Amounts *received* in the tax year from employment etc, plus the value of any benefits, less any allowable deductions.** We will examine employment income in detail in Chapter 4.

HOW INCOME TAX IS CALCULATED

As already stated, income tax is usually worked out by using an 'income tax computation' for a specific tax year. This is a calculation that simply brings together the amounts of income from the various categories that apply to the individual and shows the workings for the tax that is payable. It is important that you are able to calculate an individual's income tax, so you will need to learn the basic computation structure and practise plenty of examples. The computation can be understood quite easily if we think of it as divided into three main parts.

1   The first part collects together and adds up the income from the different categories that are relevant. It is also a good idea to note in the computation any tax that has already been paid or deducted from each of these income sources, so that we can account for it later on. In complicated situations it will be necessary to calculate the income under each of the categories separately before the main computation is attempted.

2   The second part of the computation is where personal allowances are deducted from the total income from the first section. Every individual (apart from those with very high income) has a personal allowance for each tax year. This represents the tax-free portion of their income for that year. The final figure that results from this section is known as the 'taxable income'.

3   The third part of the computation is where the taxable income from the previous part is used to calculate the amount of income tax. This is carried out using 'tax bands' and the percentage income tax rates that apply to each band. The total tax from this calculation is then compared with the amount already paid to arrive at the amount still owing to HM Revenue & Customs (or to the taxpayer). The final date for payment of Income Tax is 31 January following the end of the tax year.

Throughout this book we will use the allowances and tax bands relating to 2016/17. Whatever tax year is used, the principles and process are the same.

Full details of allowances and tax bands can be found at the beginning of this book. The majority of this data will also be provided in your examination.

personal allowance

The personal allowance is £11,000 for 2016/17. This is the amount that an individual's income can amount to in the tax year before they start paying income tax. It is always deducted from total income in the computation before the tax is calculated. Individuals with very high income (over £100,000) will have their personal allowances reduced or eliminated. We will see how this works in detail in Chapter 5. There are also separate allowances that relate specifically to savings income and dividends that apply to most people with this type of income. These allowances are in addition to the main personal allowances, and work in a slightly different way. We will examine how these allowances are used in detail in Chapter 3.

tax bands

The tax bands apply to an individual's taxable income – their total income for the year after the personal allowance has been deducted. The tax is calculated by multiplying the percentage shown by the income that falls into each band. This is done by starting with the lowest band and working up as far as necessary. The 2016/17 rates and bands are shown here:

Tax Bands for tax year 2016/17 – General Income		
Rate	**Taxable Income**	
20%	(Basic rate)	up to £32,000
40%	(Higher rate)	£32,001 to £150,000
45%	(Additional rate)	over £150,000

Note that there are other tax bands and rates for savings and investment income (interest and dividends) – we will look at these later in the book.

This diagram shows how it works:

```
general taxable income

£150,000                    45% rate
and over    -------------------------------------------------------------


                            40% rate
£32,000     -------------------------------------------------------------


                            20% rate
    £0      -------------------------------------------------------------
```

So, for example, if an individual had taxable general income (after deducting their personal allowance) of £20,000 in 2016/17, the tax would be:

£ 20,000 x 20%   =   £4,000.00

Remember that 'income' can include not only earnings from a job but also other forms of income.

The total income tax relating to a tax year is often referred to as the 'Income Tax Liability'. We will now use a Case Study to show the full process for a simple tax computation.

Case Study

SHELLEY BEECH:
BASIC INCOME TAX COMPUTATION

Shelley Beech works as an employee for a recruitment company. In 2016/17 she received £35,000 in income from this job, before her employer deducted £4,800 in income tax through PAYE.

She also received rent from the house that she had originally been left by her grandfather. The taxable amount of rent for 2016/17 has already been worked out as £10,500, but she hasn't paid any income tax on this yet.

Shelley is entitled to the personal allowance of £11,000 for the tax year.

required

Using an income tax computation, calculate the total income tax that Shelley is liable to pay for the tax year 2016/17, and how much of this amount has not yet been paid.

solution

Following the format discussed earlier, we can produce an income tax computation as follows:

Shelley Beech – Income Tax Computation for 2016/17

	£	£
		Tax Paid
Employment Income	35,000	4,800
Property Income (rent)	10,500	–
Total Income	45,500	4,800
Less Personal Allowance	11,000	
Taxable Income	34,500	

Income Tax Calculation

£32,000 x 20%		6,400.00
£2,500 x 40%		1,000.00
£34,500	Total Income tax	7,400.00
	Less already paid	4,800.00
	Income tax to pay	2,600.00

To understand the above computation, you should note the following:

- The tax deducted at source is noted in the column on the right. The total of this column is then used in the final calculation to work out how much of the total tax is still unpaid.

- In this Case Study the taxable income of £34,500 is more than the £32,000 that forms the upper point of the 20% tax band. This means that the entire 20% band is used, as well as some of the 40% band. The income is not high enough to reach the 45% tax band.

- The amount of taxable income to be taxed at 40% is calculated by deducting the amounts charged at 20% from the taxable income (£34,500 – £32,000 = £2,500).

EXEMPT INCOME

Exempt income is outside the scope of income tax. Exempt income will not have had tax deducted from it at source, and it should not appear anywhere in the income tax computation. You should make sure that you are familiar with the following abbreviated list of exempt income, since it is possible that items from it could be included in an examination task to test your ability to select the right income to include in a tax computation.

- Prizes are generally exempt from income tax. These include:
  - Premium Bond prizes
  - Lottery prizes (of any amount)
  - betting winnings (unless a professional gambler)
- Income from ISAs and New ISAs are specifically exempt. This form of investment has been designed by the government to encourage saving and investment by exempting the income from tax.
- Damages arising from personal injury or death.
- Educational grants.

We will look at savings and investment income in detail in Chapter 3.

We will now use a further Case Study to see how some of the issues covered in this chapter can be dealt with all together.

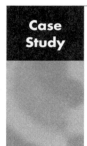

Case Study

MARK DOWNE: INCOME FROM VARIOUS SOURCES

Mark Downe is a self-employed market trader. His profits (adjusted for income tax purposes) for the last two accounting periods were as follows:

Year ended 30/6/16	£30,000
Year ended 30/6/17	£28,000

He also has income from a house that he rents out to students. The following profits from this have been calculated on an accruals basis and adjusted for tax purposes.

6/4/2015 - 5/4/2016	£10,500
6/4/2016 - 5/4/2017	£13,000
6/4/2017 - 5/4/2018	£14,000

Mark won £12,000 on the National Lottery on 15 June 2016.

He was also employed as a part time barman from 1/7/2016 to 30/6/2017. He was paid on the last day of each month that he worked, and his monthly gross pay during this time was £500. He paid £900 under PAYE in 2016/17, and £300 in 2017/18.

Mark invested in an ISA in 2016/17. This generated interest of £120 in that tax year.

required

Using an income tax computation, calculate Mark's income tax liability for 2016/17.

solution

This is more complicated than the last Case Study, since we are given a lot more information about the taxpayer's income, some of which relates to a different tax year, and some of which is not taxable at all.

The income that should go into the tax computation for 2016/17 comprises:

* the profits from his self-employment for the accounting period ending in the tax year 2016/17, ie the profits for the year to 30/6/16: £30,000
* the rental income for the period 6/4/2016 to 5/4/2017: £13,000
* the part time bar work earnings received between 1/7/2016 and 5/4/2017, ie 9 months x £500 = £4,500

The lottery winnings and the interest from the ISA are both exempt.

We can now complete the income tax computation as follows:

Mark Downe – Income Tax Computation for 2016/17

	£	£ Tax Paid
Trading Income	30,000	-
Employment Income	4,500	900
Property Income (rent)	13,000	-
Total Income	47,500	900
Less Personal Allowance	11,000	
Taxable Income	36,500	

Income Tax Calculation

£32,000 x 20%		6,400.00
£4,500 x 40%		1,800.00
£36,500	Income Tax Liability	8,200.00
	Less already paid	900.00
	Income tax to pay	7,300.00

RESPONSIBILITIES OF THE TAXPAYER

The taxpayer should always be open and honest in any dealings with HMRC. **It is the taxpayer's responsibility to inform HMRC if they have any taxable income or gains on which tax has not been paid.**

If the taxpayer normally receives a tax return or submits one online, then all taxable income and gains should be notified on the return. If the taxpayer does not normally need to complete a return, then it is the taxpayer's responsibility to inform HMRC of any source of income that they are not aware of and they will then need to complete a tax return.

For those who do not normally complete a tax return, income that has tax deducted at source (for example employment income taxed under PAYE or interest where tax has been deducted) does not need to be notified. However where no tax has been deducted from income from some source(s) then it is the taxpayer's responsibility to notify HMRC. This could relate, for example, to rent received.

There is a general time limit for notifying HMRC about sources of taxable income (called 'notification of chargeability') which is 5 October following the end of the tax year. There are penalties for not complying with this.

tax planning, tax avoidance and tax evasion

Tax planning involves looking at an individual's or a company's financial planning from a tax perspective. The purpose of tax planning is to see how to accomplish all the other elements of the financial plan in the most tax-efficient manner, and so minimise tax. Tax planning should only involve legal and ethical methods of minimising the tax liability.

It is important to distinguish between the legal practice of tax avoidance, and tax evasion, which is illegal. Tax avoidance involves using legitimate tax rules and allowances to minimise the amount of tax that is due. This could include investing in ISAs so that any interest received is tax free.

Tax evasion involves using illegal methods to escape paying the correct amount of tax. Examples would include entering false information in a tax return or failing to notify HMRC about a taxable source of income on which tax has not been paid. Those who carry out tax evasion risk criminal prosecution.

While tax avoidance and tax evasion may appear to be easily distinguishable at each end of the scale, there will always be situations that may not be so clear cut. In particular, some 'tax avoidance schemes' have been developed that may not be legal.

HMRC has stated that where a scheme relies **on concealment, pretence, non-disclosure or misrepresentation** of the true facts then this is **illegal tax evasion**.

The government has developed various ways that they hope to prevent so-called 'aggressive' tax avoidance schemes. Tax avoidance schemes need to be disclosed to HMRC, who will then investigate the schemes to ensure that they are legal. HMRC has stated that using a tax avoidance scheme marks the individual out as a high-risk taxpayer, and that this will lead to close scrutiny of all their tax affairs, not just those involving the tax avoidance scheme.

In 2013 legislation was introduced to outlaw some schemes that were deemed to be 'abusive'. This legislation is known as the 'General Anti-Abuse Rule' (GAAR). It is based on the rejection of the old approach taken by the Courts that taxpayers are free to use their ingenuity to reduce their tax bills by any lawful means, however contrived those means might be.

In broad terms, the GAAR outlaws action taken by a taxpayer to achieve a favourable tax result that Parliament **did not anticipate** when it introduced the tax rules in question, where that course of action cannot '**reasonably be regarded as reasonable**'.

This 'double reasonableness test' sets a high threshold for HMRC to prove that an arrangement is abusive and therefore illegal.

Aggressive tax avoidance schemes are certainly unethical and rely on taxpayers not paying their fair share of tax.

The key to using legal tax avoidance measures is to only use tax rules in the way that they were originally intended by Parliament. So the use of ISAs to avoid paying tax on savings interest is entirely proper, since it is in line with the original intention of the legislation.

In general, anyone who suspects that tax evasion is being carried out is advised to report this to HMRC. This can be done anonymously. HMRC advise the person reporting not to attempt to discover any more information about the suspected tax evasion, and not to tell anyone else.

In the next section we will see how the AAT code of professional ethics deals with situations where a client is suspected of tax evasion. It is important that the code is followed in these circumstances.

THE DUTIES AND RESPONSIBILITIES OF A TAX PRACTITIONER

A **tax practitioner** is someone who helps clients on a professional basis with their tax affairs. The practitioner has responsibilities both:

■ to the client, and

■ to HM Revenue & Customs

The greatest duty of care is to the client, but the tax practitioner must always act within the law.

The AAT has published a revised 'Code of Professional Ethics' that deals with these and other issues. These apply to AAT students and members. The document can be downloaded from the website at www.aat.org.uk

With regard to **confidentiality** in general, the guidelines state that confidentiality should always be observed unless either:

■ authority has been given to disclose the information (by the client), or

■ there is a legal or professional right or duty to disclose information

The Code also says that:

'Information about a past, present, or prospective client's or employer's affairs, or the affairs of clients of employers, acquired in a work context is likely to be confidential if it is not a matter of public knowledge.'

The rules of confidentiality apply in a social environment as well as a business one, and care should be taken to not inadvertently disclose confidential information. The need to comply also extends after a business relationship has ended – for example if there was a change of employment.

One important **exception to the normal rules of confidentiality** is where **'money laundering'** is known or suspected. 'Money laundering' includes any process of concealing or disguising the proceeds of any criminal offence, including tax evasion.

Where a practitioner has knowledge or suspicion that his client is money laundering, then he has a duty to inform the relevant person or authority. For those in a group practice this would be the Money Laundering Reporting Officer (MLRO), and for sole practitioner the National Crime Agency (NCA).

It is an offence to warn the client that a report of this type is going to be made about him. Money laundering therefore is not a situation where authority would be sought from the client to disclose information!

The Code states the following regarding taxation services:

'A member providing professional tax services has a duty to put forward the best position in favour of a client or an employer. However the service must be carried out with professional competence, must not in any way impair integrity or objectivity, and must be consistent with the law.'

The Code also states that:

'A member shall only undertake taxation work on the basis of full disclosure by the client or employer. The member, in dealing with the tax authorities, must act in good faith and exercise care in relation to facts and information presented on behalf of the client or employer. It will normally be assumed that facts and information on which business tax computations are based were provided by the client or employer as the taxpayer, and the latter bears ultimate responsibility for the accuracy of the facts, information and tax computations. The member shall avoid assuming responsibility for the accuracy of facts, etc. outside his or her knowledge.

'When a member learns of a material error or omission in a tax return of a prior year, or of a failure to file a required tax return, the member has a responsibility to advise promptly the client or employer of the error or omission and recommend that disclosure be made to HMRC. If the client or employer, after having had a reasonable time to reflect, does not correct the error, the member shall inform the client or employer in writing that it is not possible for the member to act for them in connection with that return or other related information submitted to the authorities.'

Dealing with professional ethics can be a difficult and complex area, and we have only outlined some main points. If you find yourself in a position where you are uncertain how you should proceed because of an ethical problem then you should first approach your supervisor or manager. If you are still unable to resolve the problem then further professional or legal advice may need to be obtained.

The AAT reference material (which will be available as pop-ups in your assessment) is reproduced in the appendix to this book. This contains extensive additional material relating to professional conduct in relation to taxation, which should be studied in addition to the above section.

RESIDENCE AND DOMICILE

Individuals that are both **UK resident** and **UK domiciled** will be subject to UK tax on their **worldwide income and gains** – not just those arising in the UK. In order to gain some understanding of the very complex rules regarding this area we at least need to understand what is meant by residence and domicile.

UK residence is determined by some specific tests that are applied to the individual for each tax year. The tests are based on facts about the time spent living and working in the UK. At one extreme, an individual who stays and works in the UK all year will clearly be a UK resident. At the other extreme, an individual who spends no time in the UK and who works abroad will not be a UK resident. The complex tests are used to determine the residence status of individuals who fall between these two extremes. The tests are beyond the scope of your current studies.

Domicile is broadly where an individual has a permanent home and where he or she intends to stay. Domicile of origin is based on the domicile of the individual's father or mother, and will become the individual's domicile unless positive action is taken to change it. This could be in the form of settling in a different country and making a will under the laws of that country. It is only possible to have one domicile country at any one time.

Where an individual is **UK resident**, but **not domiciled** in the UK they will be taxed in full on any UK income and gains. Where they have income and gains that arise overseas these non UK domiciled individuals (sometimes known as 'non-doms') will be taxed either:

- on an 'arising basis'. This means UK taxed on worldwide income and gains regardless of where they take place – just like a UK domiciled individual.

- on a 'remittance basis'. This means that UK tax is only applied to the proceeds of any worldwide income and gains that are brought into the UK. To be taxed on a remittance basis the individual must pay a 'remittance basis charge' of between £30,000 and £90,000 for each tax year. Clearly it would only make sense to apply for the remittance basis if the individual had substantial overseas income or gains which were not going to be brought into the UK.

The above is a brief summary of the very complex rules that apply in these situations.

When we examine Inheritance Tax in Chapter 7 we will also note the impact of domicile on that tax.

<table>
<tr>
<td>

Chapter Summary

</td>
<td>

■ Tax systems have been developed based on various principles. These include equity, simplicity, convenience, stability, neutrality, efficiency and flexibility.

■ Tax structures can be progressive, proportional or regressive. These terms refer to the proportion of income or wealth that is taken in tax.

■ Income tax in the UK is administered by HM Revenue & Customs. It is responsible for publishing documents and forms to gather information about how much tax is owed, and collecting the tax on behalf of the government. It is governed by statute law and case law.

■ Income is divided into categories so that appropriate rules can be applied to calculate the amount of each different form of income.

■ Income tax is calculated separately for each tax year, that runs from 6 April to the following 5 April. An income tax computation is used to calculate the tax by totalling the income from various sources, and subtracting allowances. The income tax is then calculated by reference to the tax bands and rates that relate to the tax year.

■ Some specific forms of income are exempt from income tax and should not be included in the tax computation.

■ It is the taxpayer's responsibility to inform HMRC if they have any taxable income or gains on which tax has not been paid. Taxpayers may use tax planning and ethical tax avoidance to minimise tax, but should not use aggressive tax avoidance schemes or tax evasion.

■ The tax practitioner has duties of care to both the client and HMRC. The AAT Code of Professional Ethics deals with various situations relating to tax practitioners.

■ Those who are UK resident and UK domiciled pay UK tax on their worldwide income and gains. UK residents who are not UK domiciled can elect to pay tax on their overseas income and gains on a remittance basis (ie only subject to UK tax if it is brought into the UK), but there is a substantial charge.

</td>
</tr>
</table>

Key Terms	**principles of taxation**	the basic concepts that can guide those developing a tax system
	principle of equity	the idea based on the fairness of a tax system
	principle of simplicity	the concept that tax rules are transparent and understandable and certain
	principle of convenience	the timing and method of tax collection should be as convenient as practical for taxpayers
	principle of stability	taxes should be predictable, and not change too radically or frequently
	principle of neutrality	the concept that taxes should not change behaviour – this does not have universal agreement
	principle of efficiency	the costs involved in administering and collecting taxes should be minimised
	principle of flexibility	tax systems should be able to keep pace with changes in technology and commerce
	direct tax	a tax that is levied on the individual or organisation that generates the income or profits
	indirect tax	a tax that is charged on goods or services
	tax base	the total of the income or assets that a tax can be applied to
	progressive tax	a tax which makes up a larger proportion of the income of those with higher incomes
	proportional tax	a tax which makes up the same proportion of every individuals' incomes
	regressive tax	a tax which makes up a greater proportion of the income of those with lower incomes
	statute law	legislation that is passed by parliament – an example of statute law relating to taxation is the Finance Act 2016
	case law	the result of decisions taken in court cases that have an impact on the interpretation of law
	tax year	each tax year runs from 6 April to the following 5 April – tax years are also known as fiscal years
	basis of assessment	the rule that decides what income from a particular source is taxable for a tax year – eg the basis of assessment for trading income is normally the adjusted profits of the accounting period that ends in the tax year

income tax computation	the format used to calculate income tax – it collates income from various sources, subtracts personal allowances, and calculates tax on the resultant taxable income
personal allowance	the amount that an individual's income can amount to before tax is charged – in 2016/17 the personal allowance is £11,000
taxable income	an individual's income after subtracting the personal allowance – it is the amount that is used to calculate the tax liability
tax bands	income tax is charged at various percentage rates according to the type of income and the tax bands – for example the 20% tax band for general income in 2016/17 relates to taxable income up to £32,000
exempt income	income that is not chargeable to income tax and should therefore not be shown on the tax return or in the tax computation
tax planning	carrying out financial planning in the most tax-efficient way in order to minimise tax
tax avoidance	minimising tax by legal means (unless avoidance is 'abusive')
tax evasion	illegally relying on concealment, pretence, non-disclosure or misrepresentation to pay less tax
UK residence	an individual's residence for a tax year is based on complex rules concerning where the person lived and worked
domicile	a person's domicile is the country that they intend to live in permanently
arising basis	the tax basis that applies to worldwide income and gains as they arise
remittance basis	the tax basis that only applies to the amount of overseas income or gains that is brought into the UK

Activities

Note: in these Student Activities the words 'year end' are abbreviated to 'y/e' and dates are quoted in the format '30/9/09'.

1.1 Analyse the following list of statements by ticking the appropriate column.

		True	False
(a)	All tax systems are based on exactly the same set of principles, which are enshrined in international law and cannot be deviated from		
(b)	The principle of equity is concerned with fairness		
(c)	Vertical equity means that all taxpayers should pay the same amount of tax		
(d)	Neutrality is a concept that not all tax systems adhere to since tax can be used to try to change behaviour		
(e)	A progressive tax system is one in which the proportion of income paid in tax rises for higher income levels		
(f)	A tax system that charges every taxpayer the same amount of money is a proportional system		

1.2 The following are statements made by a trainee in the tax department. Select those statements that are true.

		True	False
(a)	One of the reasons that income is divided into categories is so that the correct rules can be applied to each type of income		
(b)	When examining the tax rules for 2016/17, the only law that is relevant is the Finance Act 2016		
(c)	Every individual will receive a tax return each year that they must complete		
(d)	All income must be declared on the tax return and used in the income tax computation		
(e)	Taxable income is the name given to total income (apart from exempt income) after the personal allowance has been subtracted		
(f)	An individual with only general taxable income of £1,500 in 2016/17 would pay income tax of £300		
(g)	It is the job of a tax practitioner to ensure that his client pays the least amount of tax. This may involve bending the rules, or omitting certain items from a tax computation		
(h)	Most self-employed people pay tax under PAYE and so don't have to worry about completing tax returns		
(i)	A lottery win of over £250,000 is taxable		

1.3 Mary has the following income:

Salary of £1,000 per month from her employment throughout 2016 and 2017, plus bonuses paid as follows:

£300 paid in May 2016 re y/e 31/12/15

£500 paid in May 2017 re y/e 31/12/16

Mary had £260 deducted under PAYE during 2016/17.

Part time self-employed business – profits as follows:

y/e 30/9/16   £2,800

y/e 30/9/17   £2,750

She also rents out a property that she owns. She received £4,500 in rent for the period 6/4/16 - 5/4/17 after deducting allowable costs.

Required:

Using an Income Tax Computation for 2016/17, calculate Mary's total income tax liability, and how much of it has not been paid.

1.4   The following is a list of the sources of Sue's income for the tax year.

(a)   Dividends from shares in UK companies

(b)   Income from employment as a Sales Manager

(c)   Interest from an ISA

(d)   Interest from a bank deposit account

(e)   Winnings from a bet on the Grand National

(f)   Rent received from a property let to students

Required:

For each income source either state which category it should be included under, or state that it is exempt from income tax.

1.5   John has the following income:

- wages from employment £900 per month

- rental income from a house left to him by his Grandmother, due on the last day of each month. The £250 per month for the months of April 2016 - February 2017 were paid on time. The £250 for March 2017 was paid on 30/4/17 along with the April rent

- there were no allowable expenses to be deducted from this rental income

- interest Earned on ISA with B&B Building Society, £230

John paid nothing during 2016/17 under PAYE.

Required:

Using an Income Tax Computation for the tax year, calculate John's total income tax liability, and how much of it has not been paid.

1.6   Megan has the following income:

Salary of £2,800 per month from her employment throughout 2016 and 2017, plus bonuses paid as follows:

£800 paid in September 2016 re y/e 31/3/16

£500 paid in September 2017 re y/e 31/3/17

Megan had £4,680 deducted under PAYE during 2016/17.

Income from writing articles for technical magazines, categorised as trading income, as follows:

year ended 31/12/16	£14,700
year ended 31/12/17	£16,350

Required:

Using an Income Tax Computation for the tax year, calculate Megan's total income tax liability, and how much of it has not been paid.

1.7 Analyse the following list of statements by ticking the appropriate column.

		True	False
(a)	It is the taxpayer's responsibility to inform HMRC if they have any taxable income on which tax has not been paid		
(b)	If tax evasion is suspected then HMRC should generally be informed. If the suspected tax evader is a client then the AAT Code of Professional Ethics should also be followed		
(c)	Clients should not be advised to invest in ISAs in case they are considered to be evading tax		
(d)	A tax scheme that relies on concealment, pretence, non-disclosure or misrepresentation of the true facts is illegal tax evasion		
(e)	All UK taxpayers can choose to pay tax based on the remittance basis		
(f)	Taxpayers who are UK resident and UK domiciled only incur UK tax on income and gains that originate in the UK		

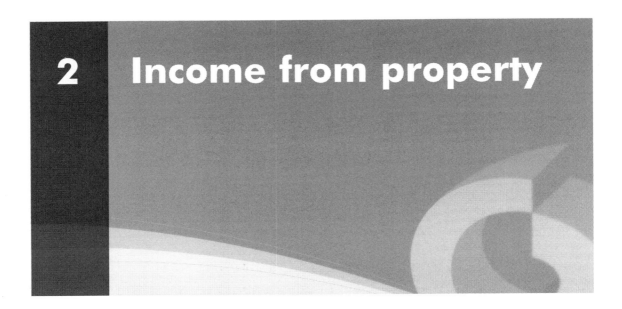

2 Income from property

this chapter covers...

In this chapter we will examine how income from rented UK property is taxed. We will start by examining what exactly is covered by the rules that we need to learn, and then see how the accruals basis is applied to this type of income.

We will look in detail at the expenditure that is 'allowable' – that which can reduce the taxable amount. We will contrast this with disallowable expenditure, and see how a calculation of taxable profit is carried out for both individual and multiple properties.

HOW PROPERTY INCOME IS TAXED

what does Property Income cover?

Property income can include:

- income from renting out land
- income from renting out unfurnished property
- income from renting out furnished property

The term 'property' is used to mean buildings, either residential (flats, houses, etc) or commercial (offices etc).

You may be asked to calculate the amount assessable relating to one or more properties that are rented out by a client. The client is usually the owner of the properties, but it would be possible for him to have rented them from another landlord. The landlord may have bought the property specifically to rent out. This is known as 'buy to let'.

accruals basis of calculation

You may remember from the last chapter that a 'basis of assessment' sets out the way that income is calculated and linked to tax years. The basis of assessment for property income is **profits** from land and property **for the tax year**, calculated on an **accruals** basis.

This means the income should therefore relate to the tax year in which it will be assessed. For example, for the tax year 2016/17 this would be the period 6/4/16 to 5/4/17.

You need to be clear about the distinction between:

- the accruals basis that we use here. (This is the same basis that applies to statements of profit or loss (income statements) under normal financial accounting rules), and
- the receipts (or cash) basis that does not apply to this category, but applies (for example) to salaries and wages

Because property income is calculated on an accruals basis, the assessable rental income is that which **relates to the tax year**. So, for example, (assuming an ongoing tenancy):

- if a tenant had paid more than one year's worth of rent during the tax year, only the amount that related to the tax year would be assessable in the tax year
- if a tenant had fallen behind with his rental payments, the amount that related to the tax year would still be assessable in that year, even though it hadn't all been received. This is provided the tenant was able to pay it eventually

One issue to be careful about is where an unpaid amount of rent is considered 'irrecoverable'. In these circumstances the irrecoverable amount can be deducted from the rental income. This is exactly the same logic that occurs in financial accounting, when 'irrecoverable debts' are written off.

Case Study

MINNIE STREET: ASSESSABLE RENT

Minnie Street rents out two unfurnished properties to tenants. Each has a monthly rental of £500, payable in advance on the 6th day of each month.

From January 2016 onwards, the following rents were paid:

The tenant of property one paid the rent on time every month during 2016. On 6 January 2017 he paid six months rent in advance since he was going on a long holiday.

The tenant of property two also paid the rent on time every month during 2016. During 2017 he failed to pay any rent. He left the property on 5 March, without leaving a forwarding address or paying the rent that he owed. Minnie has been unable to locate him since then. Property two was re-let to another tenant in May 2017.

required

Calculate the assessable amount under property income for Minnie Street for the tax year 2016/17.

solution

The assessable amount for **property one** is 12 x £500 = £6,000. The extra rent paid in advance by the tenant that relates to the period after 6/4/2017 will be assessable in the following tax year.

The assessable amount for **property two** is calculated as:

Relating to the period of occupation		
6/4/2016 - 5/3/2017	11 x £500	= £5,500
Less irrecoverable amounts (relating to		
rent due in January and February but not paid)	2 x £500	= £1,000
		£4,500

Since property two is not rented out in the period 6/3/2017 to 5/4/2017 there is no assessable amount for this month.

The total amount assessable as property income for Minnie Street for 2016/17 is therefore £6,000 + £4,500 = £10,500.

EXPENDITURE THAT IS ALLOWABLE

'Allowable' expenditure is expenditure that can be deducted from the rental income to arrive at the assessable property income.

Note that some expenditure that is quite proper from an accounting point of view may not be 'allowable' for taxation purposes. This does not mean that the accounts produced are necessarily wrong, but we will need to make adjustments before they are suitable for our tax work.

The general rule for expenditure to be allowable in a property income calculation is that it must be:

■ revenue rather than capital in nature (except some replacement items – see later), and

■ 'wholly and exclusively' for the purpose of lettings

Allowable expenditure may include:

■ business rates, water rates and council tax – this would apply where the landlord has paid these items, effectively on behalf of the tenant – the rent would have been set at such a level to allow for the fact that the landlord was paying this cost

■ rent paid to a 'superior' landlord – this would apply only if the property did not belong to the client, but was rented from someone else, the situation would therefore be one of 'subletting'

■ interest paid on a loan or mortgage to buy the property – this applies where the client is the owner; where payments are made to the lender that include both interest and repayment of the amount borrowed, only the interest part is allowable

■ insurance and management expenses

■ costs of advertising for tenants

■ ongoing repairs, maintenance and redecoration costs (but not those of a **capital** nature – see next page)

■ irrecoverable rent (as discussed above)

Expenditure that satisfies the above rules and is incurred before the premises are rented out or in periods in-between rental periods ('void' periods) is also generally allowable. However, such expenditure is not allowed during periods when the property is used privately – for example when a family member is living there without paying rent.

allowance for replacement items

From 2016/17 onwards, allowable expenditure also includes the replacement of domestic items such as furniture, furnishings, appliances (including 'white goods') and kitchenware. This only covers the replacement of items that existed in the property previously – it does not cover the expenditure on the first time that an item is purchased by the landlord. This is an important exception to the general rule that capital expenditure is not allowable.

So, for example, if a landlord rented out a property that included a cooker, the original cost of the cooker would not be allowable. If the cooker subsequently stopped working, a replacement cooker would be an allowable cost.

Where there are disposal costs for the old item, these are also allowable, but where the old item is sold then the proceeds are deducted from the cost of the replacement.

Unlike 'wear and tear allowance' which has been abolished, this allowance is available to both furnished and unfurnished property.

EXPENDITURE THAT IS NOT ALLOWABLE

Since only revenue expenditure (and some replacement expenditure) is allowable, it follows that most capital expenditure will not be allowable. Non-allowable capital expenditure includes the following:

- the **cost of the property itself** together with any initial purchase of furniture etc. Also considered as capital will be the costs connected with the purchase, including the legal and professional fees and Stamp Duty Land Tax incurred in buying the property

- the **cost of improvements**. This will apply when expenditure is incurred in upgrading or extending the property. For example, building a garage is an improvement, as is the installation of central heating where none existed previously. Note that normal ongoing repairs and maintenance when the property is simply brought back to its previous condition are allowable

- the **cost of renovations** carried out before a property is rented out for the first time. One argument for viewing this expenditure as capital is that the need for the renovations will have been reflected in the lower purchase price of the property

Other costs that are not allowable include the following:

- depreciation of any kind relating to capital expenditure

- expenditure not connected with the business of lettings (for example, expenditure on a private part of the property)

CALCULATING THE PROFIT OR LOSS UNDER PROPERTY INCOME

To arrive at the profit or loss under property income we need to:

■ determine the assessable rents receivable, and

■ deduct any allowable expenditure

The calculation of the profit or loss is known as a **property income computation**.

dealing with a single property

We will now present a Case Study involving a single property to show how this calculation can be carried out. We will use the information regarding allowable expenditure to help us (see pages 2.3 and 2.4).

Case Study

UNA LODGE:
CALCULATING ASSESSABLE PROPERTY INCOME

Una Lodge rents out one furnished property. The following is a statement compiled from her accounting records relating to the period 6/4/2016 - 5/4/2017.

	£	£
Rental Income Receivable		12,000
less expenditure:		
Council Tax	800	
Water Rates	400	
Irrecoverable Rent	600	
Insurance	300	
Installing Central Heating	2,000	
Depreciation of Furniture	900	
Managing Agent's Charges	600	
Replacement of carpet	800	
		6,400
Profit		5,600

required

Calculate the assessable property income for Una Lodge.

solution

We can re-draft the profit statement, incorporating only allowable expenditure and deductions as follows:

Property Income Computation

	£	£
Rental Income		12,000
less allowable expenditure:		
Council Tax	800	
Water Rates	400	
Irrecoverable Rent	600	
Insurance	300	
Managing Agent's Charges	600	
Replacement of carpet	800	
		3,500
Assessable		8,500

Notes

- The installation of central heating is capital expenditure, and therefore not allowable for tax purposes.
- Depreciation is never allowable.
- The replacement of the carpet is allowable from 2016/17.

several properties

When there is more than one property, the best approach is to draw up a statement with one column for each property. The addition of a total column provides a means of double-checking your arithmetic, and sets out the figures needed for the tax return. Each property can then be dealt with in turn, and the overall result incorporated into one property income assessment figure. If one property then incurs a loss after adjustment for tax purposes, it should be offset against the assessable profits from the other properties. Using a columnar format like this enables the net result to be calculated quite easily, as in the Case Study which follows.

In a later section (page 2.9) we will go on to see how to deal with a situation where the net effect of all the properties is a loss.

Case Study

ANDY LORD:
PROFITS FROM SEVERAL PROPERTIES

Andy Lord rents out three properties in High Street. Property number 1 is unfurnished, while properties 2 and 3 are furnished.

Andy has provided the following statement of income and expenditure on the properties for the period 6/4/2016 - 5/4/2017.

	Property 1		Property 2		Property 3	
	£	£	£	£	£	£
Rental Income		5,000		3,500		4,300
Less expenses:						
Council Tax	500		–		400	
Loan Interest	3,600		2,040		–	
Rent Payable	–		–		2,500	
Property Insurance	200		200		200	
Bad Debt	600		–		–	
Roof Repairs	700		–		–	
Other Repairs	2,900		450		200	
Replacement furniture	–		–		750	
Professional Fees for Debt Recovery	150		–		–	
Depreciation	500		500		500	
		9,150		3,190		4,550
Profit / (Loss)		(4,150)		310		(250)

You have also determined the following facts:

- property number two was occupied rent-free by Andy's student son until 5 September, when it was let out commercially to a tenant. The repairs were completed in December. The other expenses relate to the whole tax year

- the loan interest relates to mortgages obtained to purchase properties number one and two

- the rent payable relates to property number three that is not owned by Andy Lord

- the bad debt and the professional fees for attempted debt recovery relate to a problem with a tenant for property number one who left whilst owing rent. He cannot be traced

- 'Roof Repairs' relates to the cost of repairing damage that occurred during a storm. This amount was not covered by the insurance policy

- 'Other Repairs' includes £2,900 paid to build a porch on property number one

required

Calculate the amount of assessable property income.

solution

	Property 1	Property 2	Property 3	Total
	£	£	£	£
Rental Income	5,000	3,500	4,300	12,800
Less allowable expenses:				
Council Tax	500	–	400	900
Loan Interest	3,600	1,190	–	4,790
Rent Payable	–	–	2,500	2,500
Property Insurance	200	117	200	517
Bad Debt	600		–	600
Roof Repairs	700	–	–	700
Other Repairs	–	450	200	650
Replacement furniture	–	–	750	750
Professional Fees for Debt Recovery	150	–	–	150
Assessable amount	(750)	1,743	250	1,243

Notes

- Property number two is only rented out commercially for seven months of the tax year. Therefore only 7/12 of the loan interest and 7/12 of the property insurance expenses are allowable.

- The bad debt for property No. 1 is considered as irrecoverable rent and is therefore allowable.

- The professional fees for attempting to recover the debt are wholly and exclusively for the rental business and therefore allowable.

- The roof repairs are allowable as revenue expenditure.

- The 'other repairs' are allowable, with the exception of the porch that is considered an improvement and therefore capital in nature.

- Depreciation is not allowable.

- The replacement furniture is allowable.

- The loss for property No. 1 is offset against the profits on the other properties to give a 'property income' figure of £1,243.

DEALING WITH PROPERTY LOSSES

Earlier in this chapter we saw how a loss when renting one property is offset against profits for other properties in the same tax year.

However, if *either:*

■ there are no other properties with profits in that tax year, *or*

■ the net result from all the properties is a loss

then the following occurs:

■ the property income assessment for the tax year is nil, and

■ the loss must be carried forward until there is sufficient future property income to offset it

The property loss can only be set against future property income. If there are insufficient property income profits in the tax year that follows the loss, then the balance of the loss is carried forward again until it can be relieved.

Relief for losses is only available if the loss arises from commercial letting – not for property let to a friend or relative at a reduced rate.

The Case Study below demonstrates how property losses are relieved.

Case Study

IVOR COST:
DEALING WITH LOSSES

Ivor Cost rents out several properties. After amalgamating the rents from all his properties, and deducting all allowable expenses he has arrived at the following figures:

Tax Year	Profit / (Loss)
	£
2014/15	(5,500)
2015/16	3,800
2016/17	6,400

required

Calculate the assessable property income for each of the three tax years referred to.

solution

Tax Year	Working	Property Income Assessment
2014/15	loss of £5,500 carried forward to next year	Nil
2015/16	£3,800 of loss used against profit of £3,800. Balance of loss carried forward	Nil
2016/17	Profit £6,400 less balance of loss £1,700	£4,700

Chapter Summary

- Income from renting land and property is assessed under 'property income'. The basis of assessment for this is the income relating to the tax year, less allowable expenses, calculated on an accruals basis. The calculation of the assessable amount is known as a property income computation.

- Allowable expenses are those wholly and exclusively for the business of lettings. Irrecoverable rent is an allowable expense, as is replacement of furniture and appliances.

- Expenditure that is not allowable includes most capital expenditure and any form of depreciation.

- Where more than one property is let, the results are combined and any individual losses netted off against other properties with profits. Where the overall result is a loss, this is carried forward against future property income profits.

Key Terms

property income	the term used to categorise income from land and property (typically rental income)
accruals basis	this is where normal accountancy rules are followed, so that income and expenditure is matched to the period of time that it relates to; property income must be calculated by using the accruals basis, matching the profits to the tax year
allowable expenditure	expenditure that may be deducted from income in the calculation of profits or losses for tax purposes

Activities

2.1   Julie rented out her unfurnished property from 6/7/2016, and received £5,000 for 12 months' rent in advance on that day. She also set up a direct debit payment of £25 per month for property insurance. In December 2016 she spent £200 replacing a broken fridge.

Calculate the assessable property income for 2016/17.

2.2   Dave bought an unfurnished flat on 6/11/2016, and immediately let it to a tenant for £400 per month, payable monthly. Dave paid £2,000 legal fees to acquire the flat, and paid monthly mortgage interest relating to the office of £150. He also paid £30 per month property insurance.

Dave used the services of an agent to collect the rent and liaise with the tenant. The agent charged £1,200 per year for this service.

Calculate the assessable property income for 2016/17.

2.3   Anna Partement rents out one furnished property. The following is a statement compiled from her accounting records relating to the tax year:

	£	£
Rental Income Receivable		10,000
less expenditure:		
Council Tax	700	
Water Rates	300	
Insurance	400	
Cost of Replacement Carpets	2,500	
Depreciation of Furniture	800	
Managing Agent's Charges	1,000	
		5,700
Profit		4,300

Required:

Calculate the property income for Anna for the tax year.

2.4   Sonny Hill rents out three country cottages. All properties are furnished.

He has provided the following statement of income and expenditure on the properties for the tax year:

	Property 1		Property 2		Property 3	
	£	£	£	£	£	£
Rental Income		8,000		6,000		5,500
Less expenses:						
Council Tax	800		650		400	
Loan Interest	3,600		2,000		4,000	
Property Insurance	400		300		250	
Redecoration	–		600		–	
Repainting Windows	500		450		500	
Other Repairs	2,900		400		200	
Accountancy Fees	150		150		150	
Purchase of furniture					2,800	
Depreciation	500		500		500	
		8,850		5,050		8,800
Profit / (Loss)		(850)		950		(3,300)

You have also determined the following facts:

- property number three was purchased on 6 June. This property was rented out from 6 July. The council tax on this property relates to the nine month period from 6 July. Other expenses relate to the ten month period from 6 June

- the loan interest relates to mortgages obtained to purchase the properties

- 'Other Repairs' includes £2,600 paid to install central heating in property number one where none had previously existed

- Sonny Hill has an unrelieved property income loss of £1,000 brought forward from the previous tax year

- the purchase of furniture for property three was made on 1 July

Required:

Calculate the property income for the tax year.

2.5   Maisey Nett rents out one furnished property. The following is a statement compiled from her accounting records relating to the tax year.

	£	£
Rental Income Receivable		11,500
less expenditure:		
Accountancy Fees	400	
Council Tax	650	
Water Rates	350	
Insurance	300	
Cost of Replacement Furniture	2,000	
Mortgage Interest	2,300	
Managing Agent's Charges	1,000	
		7,000
Profit		4,500

Maisey also had gross income of £41,500 in the tax year from her job as a legal executive. She paid £6,100 income tax under PAYE.

Required:

(1)   Calculate the property income for Maisey.

(2)   Calculate Maisey's total income tax liability for the tax year, and the part of that amount that she has yet to pay.

2.6   Simon has two properties in addition to his home, details of which are as follows:

Three bedroom house:

(1)   This unfurnished house is rented out for £900 per month. The property was occupied this tax year until 1 September when the tenants suddenly moved out, owing the rent for July and August. Simon knows that he will not recover this rent. The property was let again from 1 December to another family.

(2)   The only expense paid by Simon on the house was 8% management charge to the agent on rent received.

One bedroom flat:

(3)   This furnished flat is rented out for £450 per month. The property was unoccupied this tax year until 1 June when a couple moved in on a twelve month lease.

(4)   Simon paid council tax and water rates on the flat, totalling £1,400 for the period that the flat was occupied. He also paid insurance of £270 for the year.

Calculate the profit or loss made on each property, using the following table.

	Three bedroom house £	One bedroom flat £
Income		
Expenses:		

3

Income from savings and investments

this chapter covers...

In this chapter we examine the way that savings and investment income is taxed. This includes interest from banks and building societies and dividends from shares in UK companies.

We will learn that assessment is based on the amount received (not the accruals basis), and that income is received without deduction of tax at source.

We will then go on to see how savings income and dividend income both have tax bands that are not quite the same as the bands for general income. The income needs to work through these bands in a specific order and this is explained and illustrated. There is also a Personal Savings Allowance, and a Dividend Allowance that can usually reduce the tax within these bands.

Finally we summarise the sources of tax-free investment income.

THE BASIS OF ASSESSMENT FOR SAVINGS AND INVESTMENT INCOME

In this chapter we will examine savings and investment income and see how it is taxed. There are two types of savings and investment income. They are:

■ interest received from various sources – typically banks and building societies

■ dividends from shares held in limited companies

The basis of assessment for both interest and UK dividends is the gross amount **received in the tax year**. Notice that this receipts basis applies to most types of income, but is different from property income which is calculated on an accruals basis. The period that the interest is based on is therefore irrelevant. Amounts received include money credited to an individual's bank or building society accounts during the tax year. In most situations there are no allowable expenses that can be deducted in the calculation of savings and investment income. The interest that we will be examining typically comes from banks and building societies, but can also arise from government securities (Gilts) and various loans to organisations.

receiving income gross

For 2016/17 onwards the vast majority of interest (including all interest from banks and building societies) and all dividends will be received gross – with no deduction of tax at source. This is part of a radical change in the taxation of interest and dividends which also includes a 'personal savings allowance' and a 'dividends allowance'. We will see shortly how these allowances work to reduce the tax on most individuals' investment income.

If you have previously studied Personal Tax based on an earlier tax year, you will find that these new arrangements are quite different to what you are used to.

TAX BANDS AND RATES FOR SAVINGS AND DIVIDEND INCOME

Although the tax rates for general income are 20%, 40% and 45% (as we saw in the last chapters), the rates for savings and dividend income are not always the same as these. Instead savings income and dividend income each have their own tax rates that apply in the various tax bands.

Income from savings and dividends are the only exceptions to the general income tax rates that we saw in Chapter 1. We therefore have a total of three categories of income that have different tax rates:

■ general income
■ savings income, and
■ dividend income

General income is any income except that from savings or dividends.

The following chart (which is not to scale) shows the tax bands and rates for these three types of income after deductions of the personal allowance, and is based on the tax year 2016/17.

Tax bands and tax rates, 2016/17				
Additional Rate	45%	45%	38.1%	Dividend Additional Rate
£150,000				
Higher Rate	40%	40%	32.5%	Dividend Upper Rate
£32,000				
Basic Rate	20%	20%	7.5%	Dividend Ordinary Rate
£5,000				
Starting Rate		0%		
£0				
	General Income	**Savings Income**	**Dividend Income**	

Notice that the tax rates for dividends have slightly different names.

You can see from the chart that there is a special 0% starting rate that applies to savings income in certain circumstances, even though there is no equivalent starting rate for general income or dividend income.

The 'personal savings allowance' and the 'dividends allowance' both operate within these bands to provide further opportunities for tax free investment income.

personal savings allowance

The new personal savings allowance is in addition to, and separate from, the starting rate for savings income. It means that taxpayers with savings income that falls outside of the starting rate will pay no tax on savings income up to the following amounts:

■ for basic rate taxpayers the tax-free amount is up to £1,000

■ for higher rate taxpayers the tax-free amount is up to £500

■ for additional rate taxpayers there is no tax-free amount.

These allowances effectively sit inside the bands that would otherwise apply to the savings income and reduce the tax rate within the allowance to zero.

Where the savings income is greater than the allowance then the normal savings rates apply – depending which band the income falls into. The personal savings allowance cannot be greater than the individual's savings income, and cannot be used against general income or dividends.

Although this process is straightforward for those with not much savings income, it can become a little more complicated for others. In the Case Study that follows shortly we will illustrate exactly how it works.

dividend allowance

The dividend allowance applies to dividend income and works in a similar way to the personal savings allowance, but with only one universal amount. The tax-free allowance of up to £5,000 applies to individuals, regardless of which tax band they are in. If there is dividend income in excess of this then it is taxed at the applicable dividend rates. The dividend allowance cannot be greater than the individual's dividend income, and cannot be used against any other type of income.

using the rates and bands

It is vital when working out an individual's tax that the taxable income is analysed into these three categories, and that this analysis is clearly shown in your answers to exam questions. A specific order is followed when calculating tax on each category of income. This order is:

■ general income; then

■ savings income; and finally

■ dividend income

Dividend income is therefore considered the 'top slice' of an individual's taxable income, with savings income the middle slice.

We will now use a series of examples to illustrate how the personal savings allowance and the dividend allowance work and fit into the tax bands.

example 1

Firstly, suppose an individual has the following taxable income, after setting off the personal allowance of £11,000.

- General income   £22,000
- Savings income   £750
- Dividend income   £1,100

We can see that the total taxable income is well below £32,000, so the individual will not be a higher rate taxpayer. The personal savings allowance will therefore be up to £1,000. The dividend allowance will be up to £5,000.

The tax calculation will look like this, going through the income types in order:

General income	£22,000 x 20% (all at the basic rate)	£4,400.00
Savings income	£750 x 0% (personal savings allowance)	£0.00
Dividend income	£1,100 x 0% (dividend allowance)	£0.00
Total tax liability		£4,400.00

Notice that the personal savings allowance and the dividend allowance are both restricted to the totals of the relevant type of income, and cannot reduce the tax on general income.

Now we will look at a more complex example. The taxpayer is also a basic rate taxpayer, but we can see how the starting rate for savings can apply, and how it interacts with the personal savings allowance.

example 2

Suppose an individual has the following taxable income, after setting off the personal allowance of £11,000.

- General income   £4,300
- Savings income   £3,600
- Dividend income   £2,300

We can see that this individual will not be a higher rate taxpayer, and so will be entitled to a personal savings allowance of up to £1,000.

We will work up through the types of income, working out the tax as we go.

General income	£4,300 x 20% (all at the basic rate)	£860.00
Savings income	£700 x 0% (using the starting rate)	£0.00
	£1,000 x 0% (personal savings allowance)	£0.00
	£1,900 x 20% (the rest of the £3,600)	£ 380.00
	£3,600	
Dividend income	£2,300 x 0% (dividend allowance)	£0.00
Total tax liability		£1,240.00

Notice that we use the cumulative income to work out how much of the starting rate for savings can be used. The personal savings allowance is then applied to savings income that would otherwise be in the basic rate band – the allowance is not wasted by applying to the starting rate 0% band.

The following diagram (which is not to scale) illustrates the process, and concentrates on the starting and basic rate bands.

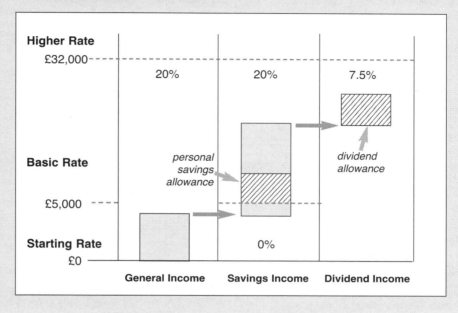

This third example is a little more complex, and involves the use of the higher rate as well as the basic rate bands.

example 3

Suppose someone has £70,000 taxable income (after deducting the personal allowance of £11,000), made up as follows for 2016/17:

- General income £25,000
- Savings income £12,000
- Dividend income £33,000

The bands would be worked through, incorporating the personal savings allowance and dividend allowance as we progress.

We can see immediately that this individual is a higher rate taxpayer since the taxable income is well above £32,000, but not as high as £150,000. The personal saving allowance will therefore be £500 and the dividend allowance will be £5,000. Since the savings and dividends received are above these figures tax will become due on the excess income.

The band levels apply to the whole income (including that covered by the personal savings allowance and dividend allowance), so that each time we move into the next type of income we use the cumulative income to determine the rate.

In our example this will work as follows:

General income	£25,000 x 20% (all at the basic rate)	£5,000.00
Savings income	£500 x 0% (personal savings allowance)	£0.00
	£6,500 x 20% (up to cumulative £32,000)	£1,300.00
	£5,000 x 40% (the rest of the savings income)	£2,000.00
	£12,000	
Dividend income	£5,000 x 0% (dividend allowance)	£0.0
	£28,000 x 32.5% (the rest of the dividends)	£9,100.00
	£33,000	
Total tax liability		£17,400.00

Notice that in this example part of the savings income is taxed at the higher rate, and the excess dividend income over the dividend allowance is taxed at the dividend upper rate.

The diagram on the next page (which is not to scale) illustrates how the system works, using the figures for the third example shown above. We have ignored the Additional Rate band in this diagram as the income is not high enough to use it. Notice how the bar representing each type of income starts at the level that the previous one ended. This is the key to understanding the system.

The personal allowance is normally deducted from the general income when analysing the taxable income. If there is insufficient general income to do this then the savings income is used, and finally dividend income.

The starting rate of 0% for savings income will only apply if the taxable general income is less than £5,000.

To summarise:

- always work up the bands, following the order:
  - general income
  - savings income
  - dividend income
- incorporate the personal savings allowance and the dividends allowance in the bands
- always use the cumulative taxable income totals to determine the bands

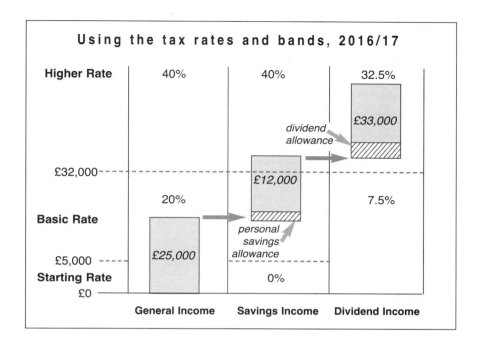

We can now use a Case Study to look at a more comprehensive income tax computation.

This Case Study does not refer to or use the Additional Rate band, since the taxable income is below £150,000. In Chapter 5 we will see how this band is used and also the impact of the changes to the personal allowance for those with high incomes.

Case Study

ANNE INVESTOR: INCOME TAX COMPUTATION

Anne Investor has the following income in 2016/17.

- Employment income of £25,000 from which £2,800 has been deducted in tax under PAYE
- Interest from bank and building society accounts totalling £16,250 (received gross)
- Dividends received of £22,500

Anne is entitled to the personal allowance of £11,000.

required

Using an income tax computation, calculate the income tax liability for 2016/17, and the amount of tax that has not yet been paid.

solution

Income Tax Computation

	Income	Tax Paid
	£	£
Employment Income	25,000	2,800
Savings Income	16,250	0
Dividend Income	22,500	0
Total Income	63,750	2,800
Less Personal Allowance	11,000	
Taxable Income	52,750	

Analysis of Taxable Income:

General Income (£25,000 - £11,000)	£14,000
Savings Income	£16,250
Dividend Income	£22,500
	£52,750

Income Tax Calculation:

	£	£
General Income:		
£14,000 x 20% (all in basic rate band)		2,800.00
Savings Income:		
£500 x 0% (personal savings allowance)	0.00	
£15,750 x 20% (all in basic rate band)	3,150.00	
£16,250		3,150.00
Dividend Income:		
£5,000 x 0% (dividend allowance)	0.00	
£17,500 x 32.5% (all in dividend upper rate)	5,687.50	
£22,500		5,687.50
Income Tax Liability		11,637.50
Less Paid		2,800.00
Income Tax to be paid		8,837.50

Notice how the dividend income within the dividend allowance pushes the excess cumulative income over £32,000 and means that it is taxed at the dividend upper rate.

The diagram on the next page illustrates the situation.

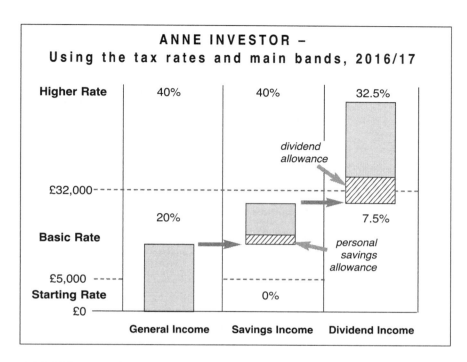

ANNE INVESTOR –
Using the tax rates and main bands, 2016/17

	General Income	Savings Income	Dividend Income
Higher Rate	40%	40%	32.5%
Basic Rate	20%		7.5%
Starting Rate		0%	

£32,000

£5,000

£0

dividend allowance

personal savings allowance

ASSESSMENT SUMMARY

As you can see, the income tax computation in the Case Study is more complicated than the calculations that we saw in the earlier chapters. The way the tax is calculated for each category of income by working up through the bands is illustrated in the chart shown above. Make sure that you can follow the logic, since it is very important for your success in this Unit that you can carry out computations like this accurately.

TAX-FREE INVESTMENT INCOME

Some specific types of investment income are exempt from income tax. You may recall that this was referred to in Chapter 1. The implications of having tax-free investment income are that:

■ the tax-free income is not included in the income tax computation, and

■ the tax-free income does not use up the personal savings allowance

This is quite separate from normal savings income that falls into the 0% band that we have already examined.

individual savings accounts (ISAs)

You need to understand what individual savings accounts (ISAs) are and how they operate. These accounts provide income which is exempt from income tax. The accounts are also exempt from capital gains tax.

Investment can be in 'stocks and shares' and/or 'cash' ISAs and are limited to a maximum total investment of £15,240 in 2016/17. There are no restrictions on how much can be invested in each category within this overall limit, and amounts invested in one category can subsequently be moved to the other (subject to the age of the individual – see below).

For example, £15,240 could be invested in a 'stocks and shares ISA' in 2016/17, and subsequently all of it could be moved during the tax year to a 'cash ISA'. The same ability to move between cash and stocks and shares also applies in 2016/17 to investments made in ISAs before this tax year.

There is no statutory minimum period of investment or minimum amount of investment in any type of ISA.

ISAs can only be held in one person's name – joint accounts are not permitted.

Each individual can only put money into one cash ISA and one stocks and shares ISA in a tax year. However in different tax years, investment could be made with different providers. There are no limits on the number of different ISAs one can hold over time.

cash ISAs

Cash ISAs are effectively special accounts, mainly offered by banks or building societies. These accounts pay interest tax-free. Once an investment is made into an ISA the income remains tax free in subsequent tax years.

If a withdrawal is made from a cash ISA the amount cannot be reinvested without it counting as part of that year's maximum investment. Therefore if the maximum had already been invested the withdrawn amount could not be reinvested during that tax year.

Cash ISAs can be transferred to another provider (for example if interest rates are better), but this must be carried out by contacting the new provider who will organise the transfer. If an amount is simply withdrawn from an existing ISA account it will lose its tax-free status.

Investment in cash ISAs can be made by UK resident individuals who are aged 16 or over during the tax year.

stocks and shares ISAs

Stocks and shares ISAs are effectively tax-free 'wrappers' for investments including shares in listed companies and government securities (gilts).

Investment in stocks and shares ISAs can be made by UK resident individuals who are aged 18 or over.

Chapter Summary

■ Interest and dividends are categorised as 'Savings and Investment Income'. The basis of assessment is the gross amounts received in the tax year. Dividends are also received gross.

■ Savings income and dividend income are both taxed at different rates from general income. The rates for savings income are 0%, 20%, 40% and 45%, while the rates for dividend income are 7.5%, 32.5% and 38.1%. Dividend income is considered the top slice of an individual's income, with savings income forming the next slice. This means that great care must be taken when calculating an individual's tax liability if income of these types is included.

■ The personal savings allowance is available at up to £1,000 for basic rate taxpayers or up to £500 for higher rate taxpayers. The amount is used within the tax bands to charge income tax at 0% instead of the usual rate. Any excess over the allowance is subject to the normal rate of tax depending on the cumulative income. The allowance cannot be used against any other type of income.

■ The dividend allowance of up to £5,000 is available to basic rate, higher rate and additional rate taxpayers. The amount is used within the tax bands to charge income tax at 0% instead of the usual rate. Any excess over the allowance is subject to the normal rate of tax depending on the cumulative income. The allowance cannot be used against any other type of income.

■ Investment income from individual savings accounts (ISAs) is exempt from income tax. There are various rules concerning investments in ISAs.

Key Terms

savings and investment income	the term used to describe income that arises from the ownership of certain assets; it can include savings income and dividend income
personal savings allowance	an allowance that is used within the tax bands to provide tax free savings income for basic rate and higher rate taxpayers of up to £1,000 or up to £500
dividends	these are the rewards received by investors in company shares; the amount is received gross
dividend allowance	an allowance that is used within the tax bands to provide tax free dividend income of up to £5,000

Activities

3.1 An individual has the following income in 2016/17, before deducting the personal allowance:

Employment income   £10,000

Savings income   £6,500

Select the total amount of Income Tax payable from the following options:

(a)	£3,300	
(b)	£3,100	
(c)	£1,100	
(d)	£900	
(e)	£nil	

3.2 An individual has the following income in 2016/17 before deducting the personal allowance:

Employment income   £21,000

Savings Income   £1,300

Dividend income   £1,600

Calculate the amount of Income Tax that is payable on:

(a)   savings income, and

(b)   dividend income

3.3 Sophie had the following income in 2016/17:

Income from Employment (gross amount)	£28,500
Building Society Interest (amount received)	£1,500
Dividends from UK Companies (amount received)	£4,000
Property Income (agreed assessable amount)	£1,900

Sophie had income tax deducted under PAYE of £3,500. She is entitled to the personal allowance of £11,000.

Required:

Prepare Sophie's Income Tax Computation for the tax year, including calculations of her total income tax liability, and the part of this amount that has yet to be paid.

3.4 Brian had the following income in 2016/17:

Salary of £1,200 per month (gross) from his employment.

Dividends from UK companies (amount received)	£5,500
Bank Deposit Account Interest (amount received)	£2,000

Brian had £680 deducted during 2016/17 under PAYE. He is entitled to a personal allowance of £11,000.

Required:

Prepare Brian's Income Tax Computation for the tax year, including calculations of his total income tax liability, and the part of this amount that has yet to be paid, or refunded.

3.5 Major Player had part-time employment income of £5,000 (gross) in 2016/17, on which he paid no tax under PAYE. He has provided you with the following details of the amounts that he has received from his investments. He is entitled to a personal allowance of £11,000.

Date Received	Details	Amount Rec'd
		£
31/3/2016	Osborne Bank Deposit Account Interest	190.00
31/5/2016	Dividend from Growth plc	4,000.00
30/6/2016	3.5% War Loan Interest ('Gilt') (received gross)	1,500.00
30/9/2016	Interest from Nationside cash ISA	300.00
31/1/2017	Bank of Northumberland Deposit A/C Interest	11,875.00
31/3/2017	Osborne Bank Deposit Account Interest	750.00
30/6/2017	Dividend from Growth plc	1,600.00

Required:

(a) Produce schedules of the amounts of savings and dividend income assessable in the tax year.

(b) Prepare an Income Tax Computation for the tax year, including calculations of his total income tax liability.

3.6 Individual savings accounts (ISAs) are subject to various rules. Select from the following, the rules that apply in 2016/17.

(a)	Cash ISAs and stocks and shares ISAs are subject to a maximum total investment in the tax year of £15,240	
(b)	Investment can be made in cash ISAs during the tax year with any number of providers	
(c)	Joint ISA accounts can be opened, but only by married couples	
(d)	ISAs can only be opened by individuals who are resident in the UK	
(e)	At the end of the tax year the tax-free status of investments made in a stocks and shares ISA expires	
(f)	The total invested in a stocks and shares ISA can subsequently be transferred to a cash ISA	

4 Income from employment

this chapter covers...

In this chapter we look in detail at one of the most important categories of personal tax – employment income.

We start by explaining the basis of assessment, and then discuss the difference between employment and being self-employed.

A major section in this chapter relates to benefits in kind. These are non-cash rewards for employees and the rules for calculating the assessable amounts are rather complicated. We will examine the rules that apply to company cars and their fuel, cheap loans, living accommodation and the provision of various other assets and benefits. We will also list benefits that are exempt from any tax charge.

We then move on to a section about expenses. These are payments that an employee makes in connection with his employment that may be reimbursed by his employer. We will examine the rules about when such expenses can be treated as an allowable deduction in the calculation of assessable employment income.

Finally we will see how to calculate National Insurance Contributions (NICs) relating to employees and employers.

THE BASIS OF ASSESSMENT FOR EMPLOYMENT INCOME

Income from employment is assessed under 'Employment, Pensions and Social Security Income', and the income tax is normally collected through Pay-As-You-Earn (PAYE). We will generally include this in the income tax computation simply as 'employment income'. The basis of assessment is:

	gross income **received** in the tax year
plus	the assessable value of any benefits in kind,
less	any allowable deductions
equals	assessable income from employment

You will notice that (like savings and investment income) we are using a **cash basis** to determine which tax year any receipts are linked to, not an accruals basis. The period in which the income was earned may therefore not always be the one in which it is assessed; this could apply for example to commissions or bonuses that are earned in one period, but paid to the employee in a later one. You should therefore disregard any reference to the period in which employment income was earned, and concentrate just on when it was received. The only exception to this rule is the rare situation when an employee becomes entitled to income but chooses to receive it at a later date. In this case it is taxable in the tax year in which the employee is entitled to the income. As well as income from current employment, this category of income also includes pensions received and certain social security benefits.

employment and self-employment

The income from employment includes salaries, wages, bonuses, commissions, fees and gratuities (tips) where they relate to a job or office. It is important to distinguish between the concept of being employed (and having employment income) and being self-employed, the income from which is assessed as 'trading income'. Employment income results from an employment contract (even an implied one) where the employer exerts control over the employee. A self-employed person or contractor has much more control over the way he or she operates.

The distinction is whether the contract that applies is one **of service** (when the person is an **employee**), or a contract **for services** (a **self-employed** relationship). These can be confusing phrases, but if you think a contract

- **of service** could apply to a servant (where the employee serves the employer)

- **for services** could apply to someone who invoices 'for services rendered' and is self employed

In some cases it can be difficult to establish whether the person is employed or self employed, and HMRC have produced leaflets and an online 'Employment Status Indicator' tool to help.

The following are indicators that help provide evidence in one direction or the other.

Indicators of Employment	Indicators of Self Employment
Need to do the work yourself	Can employ helper or substitute
Told how, where and when to do work	Decide yourself how, when and where to do work
Work set hours and paid regular wage with sick pay and holidays	Choose work hours and invoice for work done
No risk of capital or losses	Risk own capital and bear losses from work that is not to standard
Employer provides equipment	Provide own equipment
Work for one employer (but sometimes more)	Work for several people or organisations

BENEFITS IN KIND

You will have noticed that employment income includes the assessable value of '**benefits in kind**'. This is the term used to describe any reward that an employee receives because of his employment that is not paid in money. It can therefore apply to a range of 'non-cash' items ranging from use of a company car to holidays paid for by the employer.

There are some situations where a payment on behalf of an employee may count as a benefit in kind, but the expense incurred would also be considered an **allowable deduction**, thereby cancelling out the effect of any tax charge. We will examine these situations in the 'allowable deductions' section later in this chapter.

Originally, benefits were assessed based on the cash cost to the employer of providing the employee with the benefit. While this rule is still used in some situations, there are now many types of benefit where specific rules are used to calculate the assessable amounts. Through this section we will now look at the more important benefits and how they are assessed. Although this is a complicated area you must learn how to deal with all these examples, as they are popular examination topics.

company cars

A car owned (or leased) by the employer, but available for both business and private use by an employee is an assessable benefit. Most company cars have at least some private use, since the journey to and from work is considered private rather than business mileage. The way that the benefit is calculated is very specific, and is divided into two separate types of benefit:

- **a scale charge for having private use of the car** – the assessable amount is a percentage of the car's list price, and is deemed to include all the costs of the car, except fuel. It therefore includes road tax, insurance, repairs and servicing etc, and none of these costs are assessable separately

- **a scale charge for using fuel for private motoring** if this is paid for by the employer

We will describe the two benefits in turn.

scale charges for private use of cars

The scale charge for having use of the car depends on:

- the list price of the car when new, and
- the car's carbon dioxide emissions, measured in grams per kilometre (g/km), and
- whether the car is petrol or diesel

The system works by using percentages linked to emission levels. The appropriate percentage (up to 37%) is then applied to the list price of the car when new, and the result forms the assessable amount of the benefit. The higher the emissions, therefore, the higher the percentage and the higher the taxable benefit. The percentages change from time to time, since it is expected that typical emission levels will generally fall as new models are introduced.

For 2016/17 the charge for petrol or electric cars (or petrol-electric hybrid cars) works as follows:

- for cars with emissions from 0 g/km to 50 g/km (inclusive) the charge is 7%
- for cars with emissions of 51 g/km to 75 g/km the charge is 11% of the list price
- for cars between 76 g/km and 94 g/km the charge is 15%
- for cars of 95 g/km or more the charge is 16%, rising by 1% for every 5 g/km over the 95 g/km level, up to a maximum of 37%

So, for example, cars with emissions of 105 g/km would have a charge of 18% of list price, and cars with emissions of 110 g/km would have a charge of 19%.

Before calculating the percentage, the car's emission level (if above 95) is rounded down to a multiple of 5 (eg 199 would be rounded down to 195).

example

If an employee is provided with a petrol engine car with a list price of £20,000, and an emission level of 153 g/km throughout 2016/17, then the assessable benefit would be calculated as:

Percentage: 16% + (1% x (150 – 95) / 5)

                    = 16% + 11%   = 27%.

The 27% is then multiplied by the list price of the car:

Benefit: £20,000 x 27% = £5,400.

The percentages that apply to diesel cars (and diesel-electric hybrid cars) are 3% more than those for petrol powered cars. This is because diesel cars naturally have slightly lower emission levels than similar petrol models. The lowest percentage charge for a diesel car is therefore 7% + 3% = 10%.

Both petrol and diesel cars are subject to a maximum percentage of 37%.

example

If an employee is provided with a diesel engine car with a list price of £15,000, and an emission level of 172 grams per kilometre throughout 2016/17, then the assessable benefit would be:

£15,000 x (16% + 15% + 3% = 34%) = £5,100.

You will need to remember how to carry out the calculations for petrol and diesel cars.

The benefit of 7% applies to 'zero emission' cars (for example, powered solely by electricity) as well as to cars with an emission level of 50 g/km or lower. These would typically be 'plug-in' hybrid cars.

The figure calculated is adjusted in the following circumstances:

■ where the car is not available to the employee for the whole tax year, the assessable amount is time-apportioned – this is a common adjustment in examination tasks. Note that for a period of time to count when the car is 'unavailable' it must be a continuous period of 30 days or more. So, for example, if a car could not be used because it was being repaired for 25 days then there would be no time-apportionment

■ where the employee makes a **revenue** contribution to the employer for the use of the car, this is deducted from the assessable amount that would otherwise apply

■ where the employee makes a **capital** contribution towards the cost of the car, this contribution, up to a maximum of £5,000, is deducted from the list price before the appropriate percentage is applied

- where accessories or modifications are added to the car before or at the time that the car is first made available to the employee their cost is added to the list price. This would not apply however to equipment to enable a disabled person to use the car, nor to equipment which is necessary for the use of the car in the performance of the employee's duties (for example a tow bar if the employee was required to tow a trailer for his job). There is also an exception for the provision of special security equipment (e.g. bullet resistant glass) where it is necessary due to the employee's role

- where accessories are added to the car later on these are added to the list price and applied to the whole tax year in which they were added. This only applies however to accessories that cost more than £100 each (or per set)

- where the company car is a 'classic' car over 15 years old at the end of the tax year and has a market value which is both over £15,000 and exceeds the list price, then the market value is used instead of the list price

- where an employee is provided with a chauffeur in addition to a company car, the cost of the chauffeur forms an additional assessable benefit

example

An employee was provided with a petrol engine company car for the whole of 2016/17. The list price of the car was £25,000, and emissions were 123 g/km. The employee made a capital contribution towards the cost of the car of £7,000. In September 2016 the company paid for a set of 4 alloy wheels for the car. They cost £95 each.

The list price would be increased by the cost of the set of alloy wheels of £380 (applicable for the whole tax year), and there would be a deduction from the list price relating to the employee's capital contribution, but this would be limited to £5,000. The assessable benefit would therefore be:

£20,380 x (16% + 5% = 21%) = £4,279 (rounded down)

fuel benefit for private use of company cars

When an employee is provided with a company car, the employer may agree to pay for the fuel (petrol or diesel) that the employee uses for private mileage as well as for business use. If this happens, a further assessable benefit arises, calculated as follows:

In **2016/17** the same percentage as is applied to the car (based on its emissions), is multiplied by a fixed amount of £22,200.

---

example

If an employee is provided with a petrol engine car with a list price of £20,000, and an emission level of 153 g/km throughout 2016/17, then the assessable **fuel benefit** would be:

£22,200 x 27% = £5,994 (by applying the emission percentage to the fixed amount of £22,200).

The fuel charge is time-apportioned if the car, for which private fuel is provided, is not available for the whole tax year. The same rule regarding a car being unavailable for at least 30 days applies to fuel as well as use of the car. Note however that the same fuel charge applies if the employee has **any** fuel provided for private mileage, no matter how little or how much. Unlike the car benefit itself, making a contribution to the employer will have no effect on the assessable benefit for fuel. The only way for an employee to avoid the charge is to pay privately (or reimburse the employer) for **all** private fuel that has been used.

Note that for cars that run exclusively on electricity (and have 0% g/km CO_2) there is no fuel benefit charge.

pool cars

Pool cars are cars whose use is shared amongst employees for business purposes. There is no assessable benefit for employees who use pool cars, but the definition of a pool car is strict. To qualify as a non-assessable pool car it must:

- be primarily used for business purposes and any private use must be incidental
- be used by several employees, and
- not normally be kept at an employee's home

vans

Where an employer provides a small van that can be used privately there is a scale charge. The assessable benefit for 2016/17 is £3,170. This amount does not include any private fuel, which is assessed separately – currently based on an amount of £598 per year. Where the employee uses the van privately only for travel between home and work and insignificant other private use, this will not be classed as a benefit.

If a van is 'zero emission' (for example powered solely by electricity) then the assessable benefit for private use is 20% of the normal amount (ie £634) but there is no assessable benefit for fuel in the form of electricity.

cheap (or 'beneficial') loans

Where a loan is granted to an employee and charged at less than the HM Revenue & Customs official interest rate, there may be an assessable benefit.

This official rate was 3.00% pa at the time that this book was published. This rate does change from time to time. You will be provided with the current official rate in an examination, which must be used to gain maximum marks.

The benefit is calculated as the difference between the interest charge that would be generated by using the official rate, and the actual interest charged. However, there is no assessable benefit if the loan (or total loans) outstanding is £10,000 or less throughout the tax year 2016/17.

There is also no assessable benefit for a loan (of any amount) that is used entirely to purchase equipment (but not cars etc) for wholly business use.

If a loan (of any amount) is written-off by the employer then the whole amount is assessable.

example

An employer provides his employee with a £15,000 loan at an interest rate of 2% per year.

The actual interest charge would be £300 per year, assuming no capital repayments.

The assessable benefit would therefore be (£15,000 x 3.00%) minus £300 = £150.

The above example was based on a simple situation where the same amount was outstanding for the whole tax year. Where examples are more complex, with part repayments being made there are two calculation methods which HMRC will accept:

■ the first method is to calculate **exactly** the interest figures based on the balances owed for each proportion of the year

■ the second is a simple **average** method which we will explain below. This is the method that you will be expected to use in your examination where necessary

The following method is used to work out the assessable benefit of a single loan. If there were more than one loan the method would be applied to each loan and the final results added together.

■ start with the loan balance at either the start of the tax year or the start of the loan if later

■ add the loan balance at either the end of the tax year or just before the loan ended if earlier

■ divide the total of these figures by 2

■ time apportion this based on complete months of the loan (eg 6/12 for a loan that was only held for 6 months in the tax year)

■ multiply this by the difference between the official interest rate (currently 3.00%) and the rate paid (if any)

example

John was granted a loan from his employer of £15,000 on 1 January 2016 at an interest rate of 2%. John repaid £4,000 on 1 July 2016, and then repaid the remaining £11,000 on 6 January 2017.

Balance at start of tax year 2016/17 (since the loan was taken out before this)	£15,000
Balance just before repayment (since this occurred before the end of the tax year)	£11,000
	£26,000
	÷ 2 = £13,000

£13,000 x 9/12 (months of loan in this tax year) x (3% – 2%) = £97 (rounded down)

The assessable amount will be £97

Note that in this example the date of the partial repayment was not relevant.

living accommodation

Where the employer provides free accommodation for an employee, this can result in an assessable benefit. Unless an exemption applies (as we will see later in this section), the assessable benefit works as follows:

- the assessable amount for the accommodation itself is normally the **higher** of the 'annual value' (based on the rateable value), and the rent paid by the employer (if the property is not owned by the employer)

- where the accommodation was purchased by the employer, and cost more than £75,000 then an additional assessment is applied. This is based on the excess of the purchase price over £75,000 multiplied by the HM Revenue & Customs official interest rate. This is the same rate (currently 3.00%) that is used to calculate the benefit of cheap loans as described above. See later for accommodation purchased more than six years before the employee first moves in

- the cost figure is increased by any capital expenditure incurred on the property between the date of purchase and the start of the current tax year. Any capital expenditure during the current tax year is therefore ignored for this year's calculation, but will be used in the following tax year

- the cost of any other living expenses paid by the employer would be added to the assessment (for example electricity costs). Furniture and other assets provided by the employer will also result in an assessable benefit as we will see in the next section

- if an employee does not have use of the accommodation for the whole tax year, then any assessable benefit (as described above) would be time-apportioned

- any rent or similar amount paid by the employee to the employer for use of the accommodation is deducted from the benefit figure calculated

example

An employee is allowed to live in a company flat free of charge throughout the tax year. The annual value of the flat is £1,500, and the employer also pays the heating costs of the flat which amount to £600 per year.

The flat cost the employer £100,000 when it was originally purchased, 3 years ago.

Assuming that the employee could not claim any exemption from the flat being assessable, the amount would be calculated as follows:

Annual value	£1,500
Additional charge (£100,000 – £75,000) x 3.00%	£750
Other expenses paid by employer	£600
Total assessable benefit	£2,850

If the accommodation was only available to the employee for 6 months of the tax year the benefit would be £2,850 x 6/12 = £1,425.

When accommodation is provided which was purchased by the employer more than **six years** before the date that the employee first moves in, the following applies: The **market value when first occupied by the employee** is used in the calculation of additional charge instead of the purchase price (before the standard £75,000 is deducted).

Where there have been capital improvements to the property between the date of purchase and the start of the current tax year these will be ignored if the market value being used is based on a date after the improvements were made. This is logical since otherwise the value of the improvements would be double counted.

The following examples will illustrate two situations.

■ a house is first provided to an employee on 1 September 2016. On that date the market value of the house was £400,000. The house was purchased by the employer on 30 June 2011 for £280,000 and in August 2011 an extension was added costing £50,000.

In this case the market value **is not** used in the calculation since the period 30 June 2011 to 1 September 2016 is **less than 6 years**. The additional charge will therefore be calculated using the purchase price plus the cost of the extension, and is based on 7 months occupation in 2016/17.

Additional charge:

(£280,000 + £50,000 – £75,000) x 3% x 7/12 = £4,462 (rounded down)

■ a house is first provided to an employee on 1 September 2016. On that date the market value of the house was £400,000. The house was purchased by the employer on 30 June 2010 for £280,000 and in August 2011 an extension was added costing £50,000.

In this case the market value **is** used in the calculation since the period 30 June 2010 to 1 September 2016 is **more than 6 years**. The additional charge will therefore be calculated using the market value (and ignoring the cost of the extension), and is based on 7 months occupation in 2016/17.

Additional charge:

(£400,000 - £75,000) x 3% x 7/12 = £5,687 (rounded down)

job related accommodation

For the accommodation itself to result in no assessable benefit one of the following situations must apply:

- the employee is a representative occupier (for example a caretaker)
- it is customary to provide the employee with accommodation in that particular job (for example a vicar)
- the accommodation is provided for security reasons

These situations are sometimes referred to as 'job related accommodation'.

Note that in these situations the annual value and additional charge for properties over £75,000 is not applied. However, any running expenses of the accommodation (except council tax and water charges) that are paid for by the employer will still result in an assessable benefit. In these circumstances the benefit of such costs will be restricted to a maximum of 10% of the employee's earnings from the job.

provision of other assets

Where an asset is given to an employee then the assessable benefit is the market value of the asset at that time. Apart from vehicles, if an asset is provided for an employee's private use (but remains belonging to the employer) then there is an assessable benefit of 20% of the market value of the asset when first provided.

If the asset that the employee has private use of is rented or hired by the employer (instead of owned) then the assessable benefit is the **higher** of:

- 20% of the market value when first provided, and
- the rental or hire charge paid by the employer

This benefit would apply to each tax year that it was used by the employee.

If an asset that was provided in this way is subsequently given to the employee (or he/she buys it from the employer) then a further benefit may arise based on the higher of:

- market value at the date of the transfer, and
- market value when first provided, less benefits for use of the asset already assessed

From the higher of these figures is deducted any amount paid by the employee.

---

example

An employee is provided with the use of a home entertainment system, when its market value was £1,000. Two years later he buys it from the employer, paying £100, when its market value was £300.

The benefit assessed for each year that it was owned by the employer and the employee used it would be £1,000 x 20% = £200.

The benefit assessed upon purchase would be the higher of:

- market value at the date of the transfer, (£300), and
- market value when first provided, less benefits assessed already
  (£1,000 – £200 – £200 = £600)

ie £600, minus amount paid by the employee of £100 = £500.

These calculations would also apply to furniture owned by the employer in accommodation used by an employee.

vouchers, credit cards, and other benefits paid by the employer

Where an employee is provided with a voucher that can be spent in a specified way, the benefit is the cost to the employer of providing the voucher. This may be less than the face value of the voucher.

For example, suppose an employer gave his employee a £500 voucher at Christmas to spend in a particular store. If the voucher cost the employer £470 then this amount would be the assessable benefit.

If an employee has use of a company credit card then any expenditure will be assessable, except:

- business expenditure that qualifies as an allowable deduction (see next section), and
- expenditure on benefits that are assessed separately (for example in connection with a company car or its fuel)

Where an employer provides an employee with goods or services for private use, the cost to the employer is the assessable amount. This could arise if an employer paid for a holiday for an employee, or paid their train fare from home to work.

tax-free benefits

The following is a summary of the main benefits that are not taxable ie that are excluded from the benefits included in assessable employment income. Some of these have already been mentioned earlier in this chapter:

- electricity to fuel a 'zero emission' car or van

- use of a van provided by the employer, provided the only non-business use is travel from home to work and other insignificant private mileage

- private use of a bicycle and helmet provided by the employer if used to commute to work

- travel on employer's buses which are used mainly for qualifying journeys

- disabled people's cost of travel between home and work

- the following employer-supported childcare:
  - childcare provided by the employer, for example, a workplace creche
  - provision of childcare vouchers up to £55 per week that can be used to pay for approved childcare
  - payment directly to an approved child carer up to £55 per week for childcare

  These limits of £55 per week apply to basic rate taxpayers and are reduced to £28 per week for higher rate taxpayers and £25 per week for additional rate taxpayers who begin to receive this benefit after 5 April 2011.

  Note that this tax exemption does not apply to cash payments made directly to an employee.

- an allowance to cover incidental expenses while working away from home of up to £5 per night while in the UK and £10 per night while overseas

- overseas medical treatment or medical insurance while working abroad

- workplace parking

- a loan from the employer at a low, or nil rate of interest, providing the loan does not exceed £10,000 at any time during the tax year or is to purchase equipment entirely for business use

- meals at a staff canteen – provided it is available to all staff

- in-house sports facilities (not facilities available to the general public)

- counselling services

- up to one health screening assessment and one medical check up in any year

- free eye checks for employees with significant use of computers at work

- employers' contributions to pension schemes

- mobile telephone provided by employer (including cost of calls) – limited to one per employee

- an allowance of £4 per week to cover expenses incurred by employees required by their employer to work at home

■ provision of a late night taxi to take an employee home after irregular working later than usual until at least 9pm (fewer than 60 times a year)

■ goodwill entertainment for an employee that is provided by someone other than the employer (and not connected with the employer)

■ goodwill gifts for an employee (goods or voucher for goods) that is provided by someone other than the employer (and not connected with the employer), restricted to a cost of £250 or less

■ payment of a qualifying award under a staff suggestion scheme – up to a maximum of £5,000

■ long service awards to employees with 20 years or more service (and there has been no similar award in the previous 10 years), based on a value of up to £50 per year of service; the award can be in the form of shares or a tangible asset

■ relocation costs of up to £8,000 on a change of residence due to a change in the place of work

■ retraining costs to help to get another job

■ costs of work-related training for practical or theoretical skills that you are reasonably likely to need in current or future jobs with your employer

■ costs of annual staff parties which are open to staff generally and cost no more than £150 per head

■ scholarships to employees' children from a trust fund or scheme open to the public under which not more than 25% of the total payments relate to employees (otherwise these are taxable)

■ air miles or points to obtain gifts when obtained by employees in the same way as members of the public (even if for business expenditure)

■ damages or compensation which is employment related

■ reimbursement of expenses that are incurred on behalf of the employer, or that are an allowable deduction – see next section

trivial benefits in kind

In addition to the exempt benefits listed above, there is also exemption from tax for 'trivial benefits' that meet all the following conditions:

■ the cost per employee does **not exceed £50** (or the average cost if it is impractical to calculate the exact cost per employee)

■ the benefit is **not** cash or a cash voucher

- the employee is **not entitled** to the benefit as part of a contractual obligation

- the benefit is **not** in recognition of the employee's performance of their duties

The exemption also applies to the benefits provided to an employee's family.

Examples of trivial benefits that **would be exempt** from tax (provided costing less than £50) include:

- taking an employee out for a meal on their birthday

- giving an employee a gift at Christmas (not related to their performance)

- giving an employee a non-cash voucher on the birth of their child

- sending flowers to a sick employee

Examples that would **not be exempt** from tax include:

- a benefit costing more than £50 would be wholly taxable – not just the excess

- a gift in recognition of hitting performance targets is wholly taxable

Where a benefit could be covered under either these rules or a specific rule mentioned earlier the most favourable position for the employee can apply. For example, if an employer provided two annual functions for employees, one costing £140 each and another costing £40 each, both could be exempt as follows. The £140 function would be covered by the £150 limit on exempt staff parties mentioned earlier. The £40 function could then be treated as an exempt trivial benefit.

Case Study

BENNY FITT: EMPLOYMENT INCOME INCLUDING BENEFITS IN KIND

Benny Fitt works as a Sales Manager for ESP Limited. He was employed throughout 2016/17 at a basic salary of £25,000 per year, plus a six-monthly bonus dependent on his performance. He received the following bonus payments:

Period related to bonus	Amount	Date Received
July - Dec 2015	£2,000	28/2/16
Jan - June 2016	£2,400	31/8/16
July - Dec 2016	£2,700	28/2/17
Jan - June 2017	£3,000	31/8/17

He was provided with a diesel engine car with a list price of £25,500 and an emission rating of 192 g/km from the beginning of the tax year until 5 December.

After that date the car was exchanged for a petrol engine car with a list price of £15,000 and an emission rating of 119 g/km, which was kept until after the end of the tax year. Benny was provided with free fuel for private purposes for both cars.

He was granted an interest-free loan of £12,000 by ESP Limited on 6/4/16. He had not made any repayments by 5/4/17.

Benny was also provided with a home cinema system on 6/4/15 with a value of £800 at that time. On 6/4/16 he bought the system from the company for £250, when its second-hand value was £400.

required

Calculate the assessable amount of employment income for Benny for the tax year 2016/17. Assume that the HM Revenue & Customs official interest rate is 3.00% throughout the year.

solution

salary and bonuses:

The date that the money was received determines which tax year it is assessed in. This gives the following figures for 2016/17:

		£
Basic Salary		25,000
Bonuses –	rec'd 31 August 16	2,400
	rec'd 28 Feb 17	2,700
		30,100

The other bonuses are assessed before or after the year that we are concerned with.

company cars

The assessable benefit of each car is calculated separately, based on the proportion of the tax year that it is provided.

Car one is based on a percentage of (16% + 19% + 3%) = 38%, but limited to 37%.
The assessable benefit for this car is therefore:

37% x £25,500 x 8/12 =	£6,290

Car two is based on a percentage of 20% (16% + 4%).
The assessable benefit for this car is therefore:

20% x £15,000 x 4/12 =	£1,000
Total company car benefit	£7,290

car fuel

Car one: 37% x £22,200 x 8/12 =	£5,476
Car two: 20% x £22,200 x 4/12 =	£1,480
Total car fuel benefit	£6,956

interest-free loan

Since the full amount is outstanding throughout the year, and no interest is charged, the benefit is based on the amount lent multiplied by the official rate.

£12,000 x 3.00%   £360

home cinema

In the first year (2015/16) 20% of the value is charged (£160). In the second year (2016/17) the charge is based on the original value less previous benefit, since this is greater than the second-hand value.

(£800 – £160) minus £250 paid by Benny   £390

Employment Income Summary

	£
Salary & Bonuses	30,100
Company Cars	7,290
Car Fuel	6,956
Loan	360
Home Cinema	390
Employment income assessable amount	45,096

ALLOWABLE DEDUCTIONS

We will now examine the amounts that can be deducted from the income and benefits received in respect of employment, and therefore reduce the employment income assessment. These are specific amounts that the employee has paid out in connection with the employment.

The general rule is that to be allowable against employment income, expenditure must be incurred **wholly, exclusively and necessarily** in the performance of the duties of the employment. You may recognise part of this phrase from our studies of property income; but here the word 'necessarily' is added. This means that strictly speaking allowable expenditure must be for something that the employment duties could not be carried out without – not just that the job is carried out more easily or efficiently because of the expenditure. For example, personal clothing is not an allowable deduction, even if it was bought especially for work and only worn to work. There are specific instances where expenditure is allowable outside this stringent test, but you should use this basic rule when you come across expenditure that you are unsure how to treat.

expenditure reimbursed by the employer

Where an employee's expenditure is reimbursed by the employer, if the original expenditure is allowable, then the reimbursement is exempt from tax. This means that the expenditure and the reimbursement effectively cancel each other out and there is no impact on tax.

If, however, the expenditure being reimbursed is not specifically allowable, or does not meet the 'wholly, exclusively and necessarily' rule then the reimbursement will be taxable.

We will now look at how to deal with some specific types of expenditure. These items may or may not be reimbursed by an employer.

using your own transport for business

This relates to travelling within the job, (eg journeys from one site to another) not for travelling from home to the normal workplace (which counts as private motoring). HM Revenue & Customs has published mileage rates that constitute allowable expenditure as follows.

Cars and vans:	First 10,000 miles in tax year	45p per mile
	Additional mileage	25p per mile
Motor cycles:		24p per mile
Bicycles:		20p per mile

Note that this does not apply to company cars – only for use of the employees' own transport. It may well be that the employer reimburses a mileage allowance. Where this is exactly in line with these figures the benefit received cancels out the allowable expenditure, but if it is at a higher rate the excess is a net taxable benefit. If the rates paid by the employer are lower (or expenses are not reimbursed at all) then the shortfall is a net allowable deduction. This system is known as 'Approved Mileage Allowance Payments' (AMAP).

entertaining and subsistence

Where an employee incurs expenditure on the costs of spending time away from his/her normal place of work, these costs are normally allowable. Entertaining of the employer's clients is only allowable if the employer has reimbursed the employee, and then the benefit will not be chargeable.

professional fees & subscriptions

Where an employee pays a professional fee or subscription to an organisation that is relevant to his or her employment the cost is an allowable expense. HM Revenue & Customs has a list of approved bodies (available on its website), and the AAT is amongst the accountancy bodies on the list. Where the employer pays the subscription for the employee the benefit received is cancelled out by the allowable deduction.

pension contributions

Contributions that an employee makes to an approved pension scheme are allowable deductions within employment income. If the contributions are made to a scheme run by the employer, then the deduction will often be made automatically before PAYE is operated on the balance of income. If this is the situation, then amounts shown on an employee's P45 and P60 will represent income after the employee's pension contribution has been deducted. You may recall that the employer's contribution to an approved pension scheme is not taxable as a part of an employee's income, so the employee gains two advantages if both he/she and his/her employer contribute to such a scheme. If an employer makes contributions into a pension scheme, but the employee does not contribute, this is known as a 'non-contributory' pension scheme.

payroll giving scheme

Where an arrangement has been made between an employer and an approved Payroll Giving Agency, employees can authorise deductions (without limit) through the payroll of donations to charities. This is allowed as a deduction from earnings, and the employer is able to operate PAYE on the income after the donation has been deducted – just like employees' pension contributions. The employee therefore gets tax relief on his/her donations, and the employer passes the gross amount of the donations onto the Payroll Giving Agency, and this organisation distributes the amounts to the named charities.

Case Study

AL LOWE:
BENEFITS AND ALLOWABLE DEDUCTIONS

Al is employed as an administrator by Spencer & Company, and is paid a gross salary of £22,000 per year. He makes a contribution of 5% of his salary to the company pension scheme, (a scheme that is approved by HM Revenue & Customs). Spencer & Company also pays a contribution into the pension fund of 8% of Al's salary.

As a bonus, he was given vouchers to spend on a holiday with a particular travel agent. The retail value of the vouchers was £1,500, and these cost Spencer & Company £1,350.

Al is required to undertake business journeys in his own car, for which the company agreed to reimburse him at a rate of 55p per mile. Al used his car for 7,500 business miles during the tax year, and the company paid him the agreed amounts. He also claimed £300 for subsistence allowances while away on company business, and this was also paid to him. The subsistence payments are incurred wholly, exclusively and necessarily in the performance of Al's duties.

Al pays an annual subscription to the Association of Administrative Managers (a professional body, approved by HM Revenue & Customs). This amounted to £140. Spencer & Company did not reimburse him for this.

Al also pays £30 per month to Oxfam under the 'payroll giving scheme' organised by Spencer & Company. This amount is deducted each month from his salary.

required

Calculate the assessable amount of employment income for Al for the tax year.

solution

	£
Gross Salary	22,000
less	
5% pension contribution	(1,100)
payroll giving scheme	(360)
Amount used for PAYE purposes	20,540
add benefits:	
Mileage paid in excess of HMRC approved rate	
7,500 x (55p – 45p)	750
Cost of holiday vouchers	1,350
less allowable deduction:	
Professional fee paid	(140)
Assessable amount	22,500

Note that

- the employer's contribution to the pension scheme is not included as a benefit
- the subsistence allowance is the reimbursement of an allowable cost, so does not need to be considered further

REDUNDANCY PAYMENTS

Redundancy payments (compensation for loss of employment) are not strictly emoluments, nor are they benefits in kind. The types of redundancy payments, and the rules regarding whether they are taxable can be very complex. Generally the first £30,000 of a redundancy payment is exempt from income tax.

NATIONAL INSURANCE CONTRIBUTIONS

We will now turn our attention to National Insurance Contributions (NICs) as they affect employees and employers. The first category that we will examine are known as NIC Class 1 contributions, and depend on the level of the employee's pay. They are collected through the payroll under PAYE. Although there are some technical terms to be understood, the calculations are generally quite straight forward.

employee (primary) rates

The amounts of NIC paid by employees are known as primary contributions. There are various NI categories of employees, which are labelled with letters. The most common category is A, which relates to most employees, and we will use to illustrate the calculation of NIC. We will explain exactly which employees fall into each category a little later.

Employees in **category A** will pay **primary contributions** as follows:

- earnings above the Primary Threshold (PT) up to and including the Upper Earnings Limit (UEL) are charged at 12%
- the balance of earnings above the Upper Earnings Limit (UEL) are charged at 2%

Employees with earnings at or below the Primary Threshold (PT) do not pay any contributions.

The Primary Threshold and Upper Earnings Limit can be expressed as weekly, monthly, or annual amounts. The NICs calculation will normally be based on one of these depending on how frequently the employee is paid. The calculations are not carried out on cumulative pay amounts throughout the tax year, except for Directors as we will see later. The figures are as follows for 2016/17:

	Per Week	Per Month	Per Year
Primary Threshold (PT)	£155	£672	£8,060
Upper Earnings Limit (UEL)	£827	£3,583	£43,000

You will notice that the annual Upper Earnings Limit is the same at the point at which employees with no other income would become higher rate taxpayers, based on Personal Allowance of £11,000 plus Basic Rate Band of £32,000.

The following examples will illustrate the calculation of employees' primary NIC.

---

example

Brian has weekly pay of £300.

He will pay NIC of (£300 − £155) x 12% = £17.40 per week.

Anna has weekly pay of £1,000.

She will pay NIC of:

(£827 − £155) x 12%   = £80.64, plus

(£1,000 − £827) x 2%   = £3.46, making a total of £84.10 per week.

Rashid has monthly pay of £4,000.

He will pay NIC of:

(£3,583 − £672) x 12%   = £349.32, plus

(£4,000 − £3,583) x 2%   = £8.34 making a total of £357.66 per month.

You could be asked to calculate NIC using weekly, monthly, or annual figures. You will be provided with the appropriate data.

Employees earning below the Primary Threshold will not pay any NIC. However, if they earn at or above the Lower Earnings Level (LEL), but below the Primary Threshold they will be credited with making contributions at 0%. This will then count towards their entitlement to state pensions and other benefits. The Lower Earnings Limit is currently £112 per week, the equivalent of £5,824 per year.

employer (secondary) rates

While employees pay primary NIC as a deduction from their pay, employers pay their secondary NIC as an additional cost of employing each individual. Payment is made by the employer to HMRC on a monthly basis together with the Income Tax and employees' NIC that has been deducted from employees.

We will again use **category A** employees to illustrate the calculations of the employer's contributions.

Employers will pay **secondary contributions** based on employee earnings as follows:

- all earnings above the Secondary Threshold (ST) without limit are charged at **13.8%**

Notice that there is no upper limit for secondary contributions.

The Secondary Threshold is as follows for 2016/17:

	Per Week	Per Month	Per Year
Secondary Threshold (PT)	£156	£676	£8,112

Although the Secondary Threshold figures are very close to those of the Primary Threshold, they are not identical. Remember that when calculating **primary NIC** for employees, use the **Primary Threshold**, and when calculating **secondary NIC** for employers, use the **Secondary Threshold**.

We will use the earlier examples to illustrate the calculation of employers' secondary NIC.

example

Brian has weekly pay of £300.

His employer will pay NIC of:

(£300 − £156) x 13.8% = £19.87 per week.

Anna has weekly pay of £1,000.

Her employer will pay NIC of:

(£1,000 − £156) x 13.8% = £116.47 per week.

Rashid has monthly pay of £4,000.

His employer will pay NIC of:

(£4,000 − £676) x 13.8% = £458.71 per month

'earnings' for Class 1 NIC purposes

The earnings figure that is used to calculate employees' and employers' **Class 1** contributions are similar to those 'cash' payments (excluding benefits in kind) used for Income Tax purposes.

However there are two significant differences, where amounts are deducted from employees' pay (for tax purposes) relating to:

- contributions to approved company pension schemes, and / or
- payroll giving schemes

Neither of these deductions are taken into account for NIC purposes and the NIC calculations are made based on the gross pay before these amounts are taken off.

Cash expense payments that are not taxable are generally not subject to Class 1 NIC. However, where expenses are paid that are taxable (for example mileage payments in excess of AMAP rates) these will be subject to NIC.

NIC for directors

Where company directors are paid as employees, NIC employees' and employers' contributions will apply. The following special rules apply to the NIC calculation.

Directors' NIC must either be calculated on a cumulative basis throughout the tax year, or can be calculated as normal for each pay day, but a year-end check carried out on a cumulative basis. If the cumulative NIC at the year-end results in a higher figure then this will apply.

If the same amount has been paid to the director each pay day then there will be no significant difference in the two figures. However, where the amounts paid each period are very different, there can be large differences. The system exists to prevent directors manipulating their pay receipts to minimise the NIC liability.

The following example will illustrate this situation.

example

Sophie is a director of a limited company that pays her as an employee. She received £650 per month for 11 months of the tax year, and £20,000 for the final month. Her total annual pay is £27,150.

Using the payment by payment calculation, there would be no NIC (employees' or employers' for the first 11 months. In the 12th month the employee' NIC would be:

$((£3,583 - £672) \times 12\%) + ((£20,000 - 3,583) \times 2\%) = £677.66$

This would be compared with the calculation for the year as a whole, as if it has been paid in one amount.

$(£27,150 - £8,060) \times 12\% = £2,290.80$

Sophie's employees' NIC contribution in the last month would therefore be increased to £2,290.80. The employers' contributions would also be calculated using the same procedure.

If Sophie had not been a director, her total employees' NIC for the year would have been £677.66. However it is unlikely that the employment contract for a normal employee would specify such an extreme payment structure.

employers' Class 1A NIC

So far in this section we have considered class 1 NIC. As just noted these relate to earnings excluding benefits in kind. **Class 1A contributions** are only made by **employers**, and relates to the taxable value of **benefits in kind** provided to employees.

Class 1A NIC is paid annually by employers and forms an additional cost of providing benefits in kind. There is no equivalent NIC charge for employees.

The rate of Class 1A employers' NIC is **13.8%** – the same rate as the main rate for cash earnings. There is no threshold equivalent to the Secondary Threshold applicable to class 1A.

example

For example, Rashid was provided with a petrol company car and all fuel throughout 2016/17. The car had a list price of £28,000, and CO_2 emissions of 130 g/km.

The taxable benefit would be as follows:

Use of car	23% x £28,000 =	£6,440
Fuel	23% x £22,200 =	£5,106
Total		£11,546

The class 1A NIC payable by Rashid's employer after the end of the tax year would be (£11,546 x 13.8%) = £1,593.34.

There would be no additional NIC payable by Rashid on the benefit.

employers' Class 1B NIC

This class of NIC relates to PAYE Settlement Agreements (PSA) that have been entered into by employers and HMRC. PSAs allow employers to make single annual payments of tax and NIC on certain benefits and expenses – typically those that are minor or occasional.

The rate of Class 1B employers' NIC is **13.8%** – the same as class 1A. There is no threshold equivalent to the Secondary Threshold applicable to class 1B.

NIC employment allowance

For 2016/17 employers can reduce the amount of **employers' NIC** by up to £3,000 by claiming the **employment allowance**. This can be claimed by most employers, with the exception of companies with only one director / employee. Where the total employers' NIC for the tax year is less than £3,000 then it will be reduced to zero by the allowance, and where the total is more than £3,000 it will be reduced by £3,000.

employees not in category A

So far in our studies of NIC we have examined category A employees, who make up the vast majority of employees.

The following **employees do not pay NIC on their earnings**:

■ individuals under the age of 16 (classed as category X)

■ individuals over pensionable age (classed as category C)

However, **employers of category C** employees are required to pay secondary NIC at the same rates as for category A employees.

There are also special rates for **employers' contributions** relating to the following categories of employees:

Category H   Apprentices under the age of 25

Category M   Employees under the age of 21

However category H and M employees pay the same primary rates as category A employees.

If you are asked to calculate NIC for any category of employee, you will be provided with data on the rates and thresholds.

Chapter Summary

- Income from employment is categorised as 'Income from Employment, Pensions and Social Security'. The basis of assessment is the gross income received in the tax year, plus the assessable value of any benefits in kind, less any allowable deductions. Employers are required to operate the PAYE system whereby tax is deducted from payments made to employees throughout the tax year.

- Benefits in kind are generally assessed on the cost to the employer of providing the benefit. However many more specific rules have been developed to calculate the assessable amount of certain benefits.

- Company cars that are available for an employee's private use have an assessable amount based on a percentage of the list price of the car. The percentage will depend on the carbon dioxide emission rating of the car, and whether it has an electric, petrol or diesel engine. Fuel (except electricity) for private motoring is assessed using the same percentage that applies to the car, but multiplied by a fixed amount. Pool cars are not assessable, but the conditions to qualify are stringent.

- Cheap or interest free loans of over £10,000 are assessable on the difference between the 'official' interest rate and the interest charged. Living accommodation may be non-assessable, but otherwise is based on the annual value of the property, plus a supplementary charge for 'expensive' properties owned by the employer. Other assets provided for employees' private use are generally charged at 20% of their value. There are also some specific tax-free benefits.

- Allowable deductions are generally expenditure that is incurred wholly, exclusively and necessarily in the performance of the duties of the employment. There are also examples of certain expenditure that is allowable, including mileage payments at specified rates, professional fees and subscriptions, and pension contributions. Employees can also make tax-free donations to charities via a 'payroll giving scheme' operated by their employer.

- National Insurance Contributions are paid by employees on their cash earnings above the Primary Threshold, and by employers on cash earnings and benefits in kind.

Key Terms

Pay As You Earn (PAYE)	the system that employers must operate whereby income tax is deducted at source from payments made to employees
benefits in kind	any reward from employment that an employee receives that is not in the form of money
company car	a car owned (or leased) by the employer that is normally available for both business and private use by an employee
pool car	a non-assessable car that is available for primarily business use by a range of employees, and is not kept at any employee's home
beneficial loan	a loan that is at a low interest rate, or is interest free, granted to an employee by an employer
allowable deductions	expenditure that the employee has incurred that can be deducted in the calculation of the employment income assessable amount
payroll giving scheme	a scheme whereby employees can make tax-free donations to charity through their employer's payroll system
national insurance contributions (NICs)	a form of taxation payable by (among others) employees and employers
primary NICs	NICs payable by employees
secondary NICs	NICs payable by employers
class 1 NICs	the class of NIC relating to employment earnings
class 1A NICs	employers' NIC relating to benefits in kind
category A employees	the category that includes most working age employees

Activities

4.1 James is employed as a salesman. He receives a basic salary of £18,000 per year, plus commission that is paid on a quarterly basis in arrears.

During the period 1/1/2016 to 30/6/2017 he earned the following commissions, and received the amounts on the dates shown.

Period Commission Earned	Amount	Date Received
Jan - March 2016	£1,200	30/4/16
April - June 2016	£1,450	31/7/16
July - Sept 2016	£1,080	31/10/16
Oct - Dec 2016	£1,250	31/1/17
Jan - March 2017	£1,390	30/4/17
April - June 2017	£1,710	31/7/17

Required:

Calculate the assessable amount of employment income for 2016/17.

4.2 Analyse the following list of benefits in kind into those that are assessable, and those that are tax-free.

(a) Free meals in a staff canteen available to all staff

(b) Use of a company car (including private use)

(c) Free use of a company flat by the company accountant

(d) A £16,000 loan provided by the employer at 8% p.a. interest

(e) Free UK health insurance

(f) A £2,000 computer available to take home and use privately

(g) Mileage payments at a rate of 40p per mile for using own car to drive from home to a permanent workplace

(h) Use of a 'zero emission' car for business and private use

4.3   Julie Payd works as an Accounting Technician for IOU Limited. She was employed throughout the year at a basic salary of £20,000 per year, plus various benefits as follows:

She was provided with a company car and free private fuel throughout the tax year. The car had a petrol engine with an emission rating of 120 grams per km, and a list price of £11,500.

She had use of a company credit card to pay for fuel for the car. The amounts charged to the card for fuel amounted to £1,100 during the year. At Christmas she also spent £100 on private goods through the credit card with her employer's agreement.

She had her private healthcare insurance premium of £730 paid by IOU Ltd.

Required:

Calculate the assessable amount of employment income for Julie for the tax year.

4.4   Sue Mee is employed as a solicitor by Contrax & Company, and is paid a gross salary of £28,000 per year. She makes a contribution of 6% of her salary to an approved company pension scheme. Contrax & Company also pays a contribution into the pension fund of 7% of Sue's salary.

As a bonus, she was given vouchers to spend in a particular department store. The retail value of the vouchers was £1,000, and these cost Contrax & Company £850.

Sue is required to undertake business journeys in her own car, for which the company agreed to reimburse her at a rate of 60p per mile. She used her car for 11,500 business miles, and the company paid her the agreed amounts.

Sue pays an annual subscription to the Association of Executive Solicitors (a professional body, approved by HM Revenue & Customs). This amounted to £170. Contrax & Company did not reimburse her for this.

Sue was reimbursed £250 for hotel accommodation that she had paid for while on business trips. This was agreed as necessary business expenditure.

Required:

Calculate the employment income for Sue for the tax year.

4.5   Lettie Housego was employed by Fease & Company as an estate agent throughout the tax year. She was paid a salary of £40,000 p.a., and contributed 5% of this to the approved company pension scheme. She paid tax through PAYE of £6,000 during the tax year, although she suspects that the tax code used was incorrect.

Lettie was provided with a company car with a list price of £18,000 from the start of the tax year until 5 September. This car had a petrol engine and emission level of 187 g/km. She was not entitled to any private fuel for this car, but Fease & Company paid for business fuel.

From 6 September her car was exchanged for a diesel car with a list price of £20,000 and emissions of 127 g/km. Lettie made a one-off capital contribution towards the cost of this car of £1,000. For this car Fease & Company paid for both business and private fuel.

The company pays for private dental treatment for Lettie. This cost £500.

Lettie had bought her own house through a mortgage arranged by Fease & Company. The £60,000 mortgage is on an interest only basis at a rate of 6.5% p.a.

Lettie also had dividend income of £2,000, and interest of £1,500 from a savings account with NatEast Bank.

Required:

(1)   Calculate the assessable amount of employment income for Lettie for the tax year.

(2)   Using an income tax computation for the tax year, calculate the amount of income tax for the year that is still owed by Lettie, or due to her.

4.6 For each statement, tick either employment or self-employment:

		Employment	Self Employment
(a)	Contract of service is for:	☐	☐
(b)	Contract for services is for:	☐	☐
(c)	Choose work hours and charge for work done	☐	☐
(d)	No need to provide own equipment	☐	☐
(e)	Told how, when and where to do work	☐	☐
(f)	Can employ helper or substitute	☐	☐
(g)	Correct substandard work at own cost	☐	☐

4.7 **(1)** On 6 September 2016, Kathy was provided with a company loan of £24,000 on which she pays interest at 1% per annum. The official rate of interest is 3.00%. On 6 January 2017 Kathy repaid £4,000.

What is the benefit in kind for 2016/17?

(2) When accommodation is purchased by an employer, what is the value of the property above which an additional benefit is applied?

(a)	£50,000	
(b)	£70,000	
(c)	£75,000	
(d)	£100,000	

continued

(3) Would the following accommodation be treated as being job-related?

		Yes	No
(a)	Flat provided for a school caretaker	☐	☐
(b)	Accommodation provided for security reasons	☐	☐
(c)	Accommodation provided for all directors	☐	☐

(4) Edward was provided with accommodation in the form of a flat that the employer rents. It is not job related. The flat has an annual value £6,800 and the employer pays a rent of £550 per month. Edward pays £100 per month towards the private use of the flat. His taxable benefit for the tax year is:

(a) £5,600	
(b) £6,800	
(c) £6,600	
(d) £5,400	

(5) Which **two** of the following statements are correct?

(a) Furniture provided by an employer is taxed at 20% per annum of the market value when first provided.

(b) Furniture provided by an employer is taxed on the cost to the employer in the year of purchase.

(c) Employee's private expenses that are paid by the employer are taxed at 20% per annum of the cost.

(d) Employee's private expenses that are paid by the employer are taxed on the cost to the employer.

4.8   An employee (who is a 40% taxpayer) has been offered a choice of one of three company cars, as follows:

- A Nissan electric car with 0% CO_2 emissions and a list price of £30,590

- A Mitsubishi plug-in hybrid petrol / electric car with emissions of 44g/km CO_2 and a list price of £33,240

- A Honda diesel car with emissions of 133 g/km and a list price of £30,625

The company will provide electricity free of charge, and would also provide free fuel for the Mitsubishi or Honda. Whichever car is chosen, both the car and fuel would be available for both business and private mileage.

Complete the following table showing the total cost to the employee of each car during 2016/17. Round to the £ below where necessary.

	Nissan	Mitsubishi	Honda
Benefit % Applicable	%	%	%
Benefit for Private Use of Car	£	£	£
Benefit for Private Use of Fuel	£	£	£
Total Assessable Benefit	£	£	£
Annual Income Tax Cost	£	£	£

4.9   Complete the table below to show the monthly Class 1 NIC amounts for the following employees:

George is a category A employee who earns £1,850 per month

Helen is a category A employee who earns £4,150 per month

Natasha is a category C employee who earns £2,100 per month

Vikram is a category A employee who earns £3,910 per month

Carry out all calculations rounded down to the penny.

	Primary Contributions £	Secondary Contributions £
George		
Helen		
Natasha		
Vikram		

5 Preparing income tax computations

this chapter covers...

In this chapter we review the issues already covered in this book, and bring them together to ensure that we can carry out comprehensive tax computations.

We will also examine several issues that we have not covered earlier. The first of these is the payment of gift aid to charities. These payments are made net of basic rate tax, and for higher rate taxpayers there is a further adjustment needed in the tax computation.

A similar system operates for payments to personal pension schemes, and we will also illustrate how these work.

We will then examine the tax situation for those individuals with income of £100,000 or more. This can involve a reduced (or eliminated) personal allowance as well as the 'additional' tax band for taxable income over £150,000.

A REVIEW OF ASSESSABLE INCOME

what we have covered so far

In **Chapter 1** we took an overview of assessable income, and looked in outline at how the income tax computation works. We saw that assessable income is divided into categories so that distinct rules can be applied to each source of income.

The analysis of income that we need to be familiar with is repeated here:

'Property Income'   Rental income from land and property.

'Trading Income'   Profits from trades and professions (the self-
                                     employed and those in partnership).

'Savings and Investment   UK Interest and UK Dividends.
Income'

'Employment, Pensions   Income from employment. Income tax is
and Social Security   deducted from employment income under the
Income'   system known as Pay As You Earn (PAYE).

In **Chapter 2** we looked at income from land and property, and how it is assessed. We also saw how the assessable amount is calculated.

In **Chapter 3** we examined 'savings and investment income' in the form of savings income and dividend income. Again we saw how the basis of assessment is applied, and also learned that savings income and dividend income use different tax rates to other (general) income. These different rates, and the order in which income must be treated in the computation are vital if tax is to be calculated accurately.

In **Chapter 4** we explained income from employment. This is a complex area, and we saw how benefits in kind are assessed, and what allowable deductions can be made from employment income.

The only category of income from the above list that we have not looked at in detail is 'profits from trades and professions' that is assessed as 'trading income'. We do not need to look in any detail at this type of income in this learning area, since instead it forms a major part of the unit covered by Osborne Books' *Business Tax* text. We just need to include the assessable amount in an income tax computation where appropriate (see Chapter 1, pages 1.12 - 1.14).

summary of tax rates for different sources of income

Set out below is a summary of what we have covered so far and a reminder of the type of income to decide the tax rate used for each source of income.

Assessable Income	Coverage in this book	Type of Income
Property Income Rental income (less allowable expenses), for the tax year, calculated on an accruals basis.	Chapter 2	general
Trading Income Profits (after deducting allowable expenses) for the accounting year that ends in the tax year.	outline only	general
Savings and Investment Income: • Gross interest received in the tax year.	Chapter 3	savings
• Dividends received in the tax year.		dividend
Employment Income Amounts received in the tax year from employment, plus the assessable value of any benefits, less any allowable deductions.	Chapter 4	general

At this stage it is worth reminding ourselves of the different tax rates for general, savings, and dividend income. These rates all use common bands, but we must work up through the bands starting with general income, followed by savings income, and then dividend income.

	General Income	Savings Income	Dividend Income
Additional Rate/Dividend Additional Rate	45%	45%	38.1%
Higher Rate/Dividend Upper Rate	40%	40%	32.5%
Basic Rate/Dividend Ordinary Rate	20%	20%	7.5%
Starting Rate	N/A	0%	N/A

Remember that the Personal Savings Allowance and the Dividend Allowance can reduce the rates when applicable.

If you feel unsure about how the system works, now would be a good point to look again at Chapter 3, where it is explained in detail.

Later on we will be using the mechanism described there to carry out some comprehensive tax computations. Before we do that there are a few further topics regarding tax computations that we must be able to deal with.

EXPENDITURE THAT REDUCES TOTAL INCOME TAX

When we described property income and employment income we saw that some allowable expenditure can be deducted from the income within the category to arrive at the assessable amount. We are now going to look at two specific types of expenditure that reduce the total amount of income tax. They both use the same mechanism for obtaining the tax saving.

The specific payments that we are now going to look at (being tax allowable) are paid after tax has been taken off. This effectively reduces the cost to the individual making the payment.

gift aid payments

Gift aid is a government scheme that allows taxpayers to donate any amount to a charity and obtain tax relief at the highest rate that they pay.

The system operates by allowing the payer to deduct tax at 20% from the amount of the gift. The charity then claims the tax amount from HM Revenue & Customs.

Suppose, for example, a taxpayer makes a donation of £80 to a charity. The effect is to treat the payment as a gift of £100 and the charity will be able to reclaim the £20 from HM Revenue & Customs. Such donations can be for any amount, and can be either a one-off gift or a regular payment. The taxpayer simply has to make a declaration to the charity that the donation(s) are to be considered as falling under the gift aid rules, and provide their name and address.

The tax treatment of gift aid payments in the individual's tax computation is as follows:

- unless the taxpayer pays tax at the higher rate, nothing needs to be done. The payer obtains tax relief by the deduction from the payment

- where the taxpayer does pay tax at higher rate, then in addition to the 20% tax relief obtained when making the payment, the basic rate band is increased by the **gross** amount of the gift. This gives further tax saving by moving some income from the higher rate into the basic rate

So, for our example of a payment of £80 to a charity (gross equivalent of £100) the taxpayer's basic rate band would be increased in 2016/17 from

£32,000 to £32,100. This will result in extra income being taxed at 20%, not 40%. The adjustment of the band enables the taxpayer to save a further (40% − 20% = 20%) tax. In this example the extra tax saving is £20. This makes the effective cost of the donation only £60 (ie the total tax saving will be £20 + £20). If the taxpayer has very high income then he would also benefit from the 'additional' rate band starting point also being increased by the gross equivalent of the gift aid payment. This would give an additional tax saving. We will look at the 45% rate in more detail later in this chapter.

Note that gift aid is a separate scheme from payroll giving that we looked at in Chapter 4, although an individual can make donations through both schemes if desired.

personal pension plan payments

All pension schemes work in the same general way from a tax point of view. Contributions to the schemes are allowed tax relief, but when the pension is drawn, the regular proceeds are treated as taxable.

We saw in Chapter 4 that payments to approved **occupational pension schemes** (organised by the employer) are usually given tax relief by deducting an employee's contributions in the calculation of their assessable employment income.

Personal pension plans (PPPs) may be set up by individuals who are employees or self-employed. The term also includes **stakeholder pensions** that were introduced as a government initiative, and are not dependent on the contributor being an employee or self-employed.

The mechanism for obtaining tax relief for PPPs is different from that used for an occupational pension scheme. Instead it is dealt with in the same way as donations under the gift aid scheme.

Contributions are made as net amounts − after 20% tax relief has been deducted from the gross amount payable. As with gift aid donations, the gross amount can be calculated by multiplying the net amount by 100/80. The basic rate tax band is increased by the gross amount of the taxpayer's contribution, and this enables higher rate taxpayers to obtain further relief. There is no other action to be taken in the tax computation.

Suppose a taxpayer, Tom, wanted to make gross contributions to a personal pension plan of £2,500 per year. He would make payments of £2,500 x 80% = £2,000 to his pension provider, who would reclaim the tax of £500, and invest £2,500 in the pension fund.

If he is a basic rate taxpayer, then that is the end of the matter − he has obtained the right amount of tax relief through making payments net. If he is a higher rate taxpayer then a further tax saving will arise through moving £2,500 of his income into the basic rate band from the higher rate band. This extra saving would amount to £2,500 x (40% – 20%) = £500.

We will now use a Case Study to demonstrate how this mechanism works for these two types of payment – pension contributions and gift aid.

Case Study

DEE D'UCT:
EXPENDITURE THAT SAVES TAX

Dee is self-employed, with assessable profits for 2016/17 of £38,000. She also has rental income, with an agreed income of £15,000.

Dee has various investments, and these provided the following amounts in 2016/17:

Interest	£10,000
Dividends	£6,000

required

1   Using an income tax computation, calculate the total tax liability for the tax year. Assume that Dee has made no gift aid or personal pension payments.

2   Now assume that in the tax year Dee made the following payments:
   - regular gift aid payments totalling £800 net (gross equivalent £1,000)
   - personal pension plan payments of £1,280 net (equivalent to £1,600 gross)

   You are to recalculate Dee's income tax computation to take account of these two payments, and explain how the tax relief has been obtained.

solution

Task 1   **Income Tax Computation 2016/17**

	£	Tax Paid £
Property Income	15,000	–
Trading Income	38,000	–
Interest rec'd (as above)	10,000	–
Dividend income (as above)	6,000	–
Total Income	69,000	0
less Personal Allowance	11,000	
Taxable Income	58,000	

Analysis of Taxable Income:

	£
General Income (£15,000 + £38,000 − £11,000)	42,000
Savings Income	10,000
Dividend Income	6,000
	58,000

Income Tax Calculation:

General Income:	£	£
£32,000 x 20%	6,400.00	
£10,000 x 40% (the rest of the £42,000)	4,000.00	
£42,000		10,400.00

Savings Income:		
£500 x 0% (personal savings allowance)	0.00	
£9,500 x 40% (the rest of the £10,000)	3,800.00	
£10,000		3,800.00

Dividend Income:		
£5,000 x 0% (dividend allowance)	0.00	
£1,000 x 32.5% (the rest of the £6,000)	325.00	
£6,000		325.00
Income Tax Liability		14,525.00

The way the tax is calculated for each category of income by working up through the bands is illustrated by the following chart (a format already seen in Chapter 3):

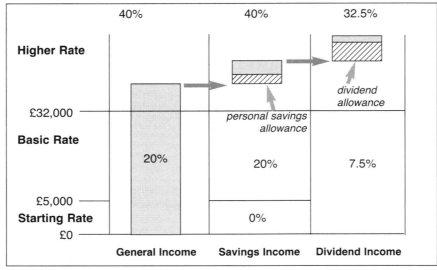

Note that in this diagram we have ignored the additional rate since it is not relevant here.

Task 2

Note firstly that the amounts payable as gift aid (£1,000) and pension plan contributions (£1,600) have only cost Dee £800 + £1,280 = £2,080.

The difference of £2,600 − £2,080 = £520 is the tax relief (20% of £2,600) that she obtained when making the payments.

The income tax computation in this case follows the same principles as it did in Task 1:

Analysis of Taxable Income (as previously):	£
General Income (£15,000 + £38,000 − £11,000)	42,000
Savings Income	10,000
Dividend Income	6,000
	58,000

Because of the payments under gift aid and to the personal pension plan, the basic rate band is now extended by (£1,000 + £1,600) from £32,000 to £34,600 cumulative.

This is used as follows:

Income Tax Calculation:

General Income:	£	£
£34,600 x 20%	6,920.00	
£7,400 x 40%	2,960.00	
£42,000		9,880.00

Savings Income:	£	£
£500 x 0%	0.00	
£9,500 x 40%	3,800.00	
£10,000		3,800.00

Dividend Income:	£	£
£5,000 x 0%	0.00	
£1,000 x 32.5%	325.00	
£6,000		325.00
Income Tax Liability		14,005.00

In this situation Dee now has to pay £14,005.

This compares with a payment of £14,525 in Task 1, a tax saving of £520 (20% of £2,600), which when added to the £520 tax relief given on the payments (see above) gives a total tax saving of £1,040 (£2,600 x 40%).

PERSONAL ALLOWANCES FOR INDIVIDUALS WITH HIGH INCOMES

When an individual has income over £100,000 the personal allowance can be restricted or eliminated entirely. This works by first calculating the individual's 'adjusted net income'. Where this exceeds £100,000 the personal allowance is reduced by 50% of the excess.

The adjusted net income that is used to compare with the £100,000 limit is calculated as follows:

Total income from all sources*	£xx
Less any grossed up gift aid payments	£(xx)
Less any grossed up personal pension payments	£(xx)
Less personal savings allowance	£(xx)
Less dividend allowance	£(xx)
'Adjusted Net Income'	£xx

*The total income from all sources is before deducting the personal allowance, personal savings allowance or dividend allowance.

If the taxpayer's adjusted net income exceeds the £100,000 limit, then the personal allowance is reduced by 50% of the difference. This means that an individual with adjusted net income of £122,000 or more would not be entitled to any personal allowance at all.

example

Jim has employment income of £95,000, plus dividends received of £15,000. He pays £2,000 per year (net) to charities under gift-aid.

Jim's adjusted net income would be:

£95,000 + £15,000 − (£2,000 x 100/80) − £5,000 dividend allowance = £102,500

This exceeds the £100,000 limit by £2,500, so Jim's personal allowance will be reduced by 50% x £2,500 = £1,250. His personal allowance will therefore be £11,000 − £1,250 = £9,750.

If Jim's income had been £122,000 or more then 50% of the excess over £100,000 would eliminate the personal allowance entirely. Note however that the allowance cannot be less than zero. There cannot be a negative personal allowance.

TAX RATES FOR INDIVIDUALS WITH HIGH INCOMES

We noted in earlier chapters that there is an 'additional rate' band that impacts on individuals who have taxable income of over £150,000. The rates that apply are 45% for general and savings income, and 38.1% for dividend income.

An individual with taxable income of over £150,000 will suffer the elimination of the personal allowance as explained in the last section. They will not be entitled to any personal savings allowance, but they will be entitled to a dividends allowance of up to £5,000. Although there is an extra tax band to use in the computation, the calculation follows the same principle that we have used throughout our studies. We must analyse the income into general, savings and dividend income, and then work our way up through the bands, applying the appropriate rates.

Case Study

HIGH INCOME COMPUTATION

Julie has the following income in the tax year:

	£
Trading income	140,000
Interest received	20,000
Dividends received	30,000

Her income tax computation for 2016/17 would appear as follows:

	£	Tax Paid £
Trading Income	140,000	
Interest	20,000	–
Dividends	30,000	–
Total Income	190,000	–
Less Personal Allowance	0	
Taxable Income	190,000	

The taxable income is easily analysed since there is no personal allowance:

	£
General	140,000
Savings	20,000
Dividends	30,000

Working up through the bands:

	£	£
General Income:		
£32,000 x 20%	6,400	
£108,000 x 40%	43,200	
£140,000		49,600
Savings Income:		
£10,000 x 40%	4,000	
£10,000 x 45%	4,500	
£20,000		8,500
Dividend Income:		
£5,000 x 0%	0	
£25,000 x 38.1%	9,525	
£30,000		9,525
Tax Payable		67,625

Note that this individual is not entitled to a personal savings allowance since she is an additional rate taxpayer.

The following diagram (which is not to scale) illustrates the calculation:

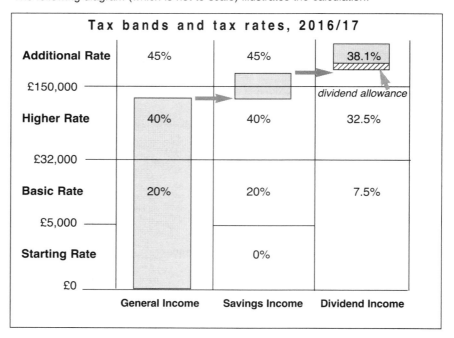

Where an individual makes gift aid and/or personal pension contributions, both the band limits of £32,000 and £150,000 are increased by the gross equivalent of the payments, and the taxpayer will therefore get increased tax relief on the payments.

example

If a taxpayer with an income of £165,000 (all general income) made gift aid payments of £8,000, the band limits would both be increased by £8,000 x 100/80 = £10,000. This would mean that the basic rate band would extend to £42,000, and the higher rate band would reach £160,000. In this situation the individual would pay tax as follows:

		£
£42,000	x 20%	8,400
£118,000	x 40%	47,200
£5,000	x 45%	2,250
£165,000		57,850

DETERMINING AMOUNT OF PERSONAL SAVINGS ALLOWANCE

We have noted that the maximum personal savings allowance is reduced to £500 for higher rate taxpayers and eliminated entirely for additional rate taxpayers (as in the last Case Study).

It is often easy to see the highest band that an individual's income will fall into. However, there are some situations where it may not appear to be obvious. In these cases the 'adjusted net income' should be used to determine the band. This is the same adjusted net income that we used earlier to calculate any restriction of the personal allowance.

When the adjusted net income is below £43,000 (made up of personal allowance of £11,000 plus basic rate band of £32,000) the individual will be a basic rate taxpayer, and entitled to the personal savings allowance of up to £1,000.

Where the adjusted net income is from £43,001 to £150,000 then the individual is a higher rate taxpayer and will be entitled to up to £500 personal savings allowance.

Where the adjusted net income is over £150,000 there will be no personal savings allowance available.

The only issue with this procedure is that the personal savings allowance will have to be estimated as it forms part of the adjusted net income calculation.

If the calculation subsequently shows that the wrong amount was used it should be corrected and re-calculated if necessary.

If, for example, you are unsure whether an individual will be a basic rate or higher rate taxpayer, firstly use the 'up to £1,000' amount in the adjusted net income calculation. If this shows income of over £43,000, then the lower personal savings allowance of up to £500 must be used instead.

---

example

Kevin has employment income of £39,000, rental income of £3,000, savings income of £1,800 and dividend income of £4,000. He pays personal pension contributions of £800 (net).

The adjusted net income can first be estimated as follows:

	£
Total income (£39,000 + £3,000 + £1,800 + £4,000)	47,800
Less grossed up personal pension contributions	(1,000)
Less estimated personal savings allowance	(1,000)
Less dividend allowance	(4,000)
Adjusted net income	41,800

Since the adjusted net income is below £43,000 the personal savings allowance can be confirmed as £1,000.

COMPREHENSIVE TAX COMPUTATIONS

We have now examined all the issues that we need to understand to produce comprehensive income tax computations. All the topics covered in the following Case Study have been looked at already in this book, and it should therefore provide a good way of starting revision.

Case Study

MAX CASE:
COMPREHENSIVE TAX COMPUTATION

Max received rent from furnished property in the tax year of £10,800. He paid out allowable expenses of £500 in relation to the property. He has £750 of losses from property income carried forward from the previous tax year.

Max is employed as a senior manager, at a basic gross salary of £84,000 per year. Out of this his employer deducts £100 per month contribution to an approved pension scheme. Max paid £28,000 under PAYE.

He is also provided with a petrol engine company car. It had a list price of £15,600 when new, and has an emission rating of 215 grams of carbon dioxide per kilometre. Max is entitled to fuel for the car paid for by his employer for business and private motoring. Max pays an annual subscription of £130 to the Association of Company Administrators (an approved professional body).

Max has various investments, and during the tax year he received £1,200 dividends from UK companies, plus £1,400 interest from his bank accounts.

Max made a £400 donation to charity under the gift aid scheme during the tax year. Max uses paper-based tax returns.

required

1   Calculate the assessable property income.

2   Calculate the assessable employment income.

3   Calculate the personal allowance for Max.

4   Using an income tax computation, calculate the total tax liability for the tax year, and the amount that has yet to be paid.

5   Calculate the employee's and employer's Class 1 NIC per month, assuming that Max is paid monthly.

solution

We will deal with each task in turn, selecting the appropriate data. In this Case Study the information is provided in the same order as the tasks to make the process clearer.

Task 1

Property Income	£
Rental received	10,800
less	
allowable expenditure	500
	10,300
less loss brought forward	750
Assessable amount	9,550

Task 2

		£
Employment Income		
Basic salary		84,000
less pension contribution		1,200
Salary per P60		82,800
add benefits:		
Company car (£15,600 x 37%)		5,772
Company car fuel (£22,200 x 37%)		8,214
		96,786
less allowable expenses (professional fees)		130
Assessable amount		96,656

Task 3

	£
Total Income:	
Property Income	9,550
Employment Income	96,656
Savings Income	1,400
Dividend Income	1,200
	108,806
Less grossed-up gift aid payment	500
Less personal savings allowance	500
Less dividend allowance	1,200
'Adjusted Net Income'	106,606

This exceeds the £100,000 limit by £6,606. The personal allowance is therefore reduced by 50% of this excess:

	£
Basic personal allowance	11,000
less 50% x £6,606	3,303
Revised personal allowance	7,697

Task 4   **Income Tax Computation 2016/17**

	£	£ Tax paid
Property Income	9,550	–
Employment Income	96,656	28,000
Savings and Investment Income:		
(interest rec'd)	1,400	–
(dividend income)	1,200	–
Total Income	108,806	28,000
Less Personal Allowance	7,697	
Taxable Income	101,109	

Analysis of Taxable Income:	
General Income (£9,550 + £96,656 – £7,697)	98,509
Savings Income	1,400
Dividend Income	1,200
	101,109

The basic rate band will be increased by the gross equivalent of the gift aid payment (£400 x 100/80 = £500).

This makes the new top of the band £32,000 + £500 = £32,500.

The income level does not reach the additional rate band.

Income Tax Calculation:

General Income:	£	£
£32,500 x 20%	6,500.00	
£66,009 x 40% (the rest of the £98,509)	26,403.60	
		32,903.60
Savings Income:		
£500 x 0% (personal savings allowance)	0.00	
£900 x 40% (the rest of the £1,400)	360.00	
		360.00
Dividend Income:		
£1,200 x 0% (dividend allowance)		0.00
Income tax liability		33,263.60
Less paid		28,000.00
Balance to pay		5,263.60

Task 5

Monthly pay £84,000 / 12	= £7,000

(ignore pension deduction for NIC calculations)

Employee primary class 1 contributions:

((£3,583 – £672) x 12%) + ((£7,000 - £3,583) x 2%)	= £417.66 per month

Employer secondary class 1 contributions:

(£7,000 – £676) x 13.8%	= £872.71 per month

TAX PLANNING TECHNIQUES

We saw in Chapter 1 that tax planning can be carried out to legally and ethically minimise tax liabilities. This involves using tax legislation in the way that it was originally intended. We will now consider practical examples of how tax planning can be carried out in connection with Income Tax. Throughout this section we must remember that tax is only one element of any financial decision – it is not worth saving tax if the decision means that other costs are increased or income reduced by more than the tax saved.

We will now consider examples based on the forms of income that we have considered in our studies.

property income

We saw in Chapter 2 that property income is based on profits from rentals calculated on an accruals basis, which reduces any opportunities for tax planning. Although all revenue costs that are wholly and exclusively for the business are allowable, it would not make sense to increase any cost simply to reduce the taxable income.

There may be scope, however, to plan the **timing** of **replacement** of assets like kitchen appliances or carpets to the taxpayer's advantage.

For example, costs incurred in the replacement of qualifying assets in March would reduce the tax liability a year earlier than if incurred a month later.

Another consideration may be the tax band that the individual was in, and how close they were to a band limit. If the individual was normally a basic rate taxpayer, but in a particular tax year was likely to become a higher rate taxpayer, it may be a good time to replace qualifying assets to reduce the property income below the band limit.

savings and dividend income

There are opportunities to invest in exempt income like ISAs, since the income will be tax free without using up the starting rate or the personal savings allowance. The amount to be invested each tax year is limited, but once invested the income will remain tax free, subject to any future changes in legislation.

Since savings and dividend income is based on the date that the income is received, there is some scope for investing in accounts that make payments at times that are most beneficial. While some accounts pay monthly interest, others pay annually on the anniversary of the account opening. Carefully selecting an appropriate account may mean that the personal savings allowance can be utilised each year.

The issue of tax bands is important for savings income, both for the tax rates themselves, and for the maximum personal savings allowance. If income can be managed so that the individual does not move up into the higher (or additional) rate then the personal savings allowance can be most beneficial.

If the personal savings allowance and the dividend allowance can be utilised to the maximum extent then this will clearly be a useful aid to minimising tax liability.

employment income

While renegotiating the terms of an employment contract is not available to everyone, there may be situations where employees are provided with options – particularly regarding benefits in kind.

One major example would be where a company car is provided, but there is a choice of model. There is a wide variety of models with different CO_2 emissions which translate into different assessable benefits, even for cars with similar list prices.

To take an extreme example, suppose a higher rate taxpayer had the choice of a diesel car with emissions of 185 g/km or an electric car with zero CO_2 emissions, both costing £35,000. If we also assume that diesel or electricity was also provided free, the assessable benefits would work out as follows:

- diesel car (37% x £35,000) + (37% x £22,200)   = £21,164
- electric car (7% x £35,000) + 0   = £2,450

The difference in assessable benefit would give a tax saving of £7,485.60 over the tax year for the electric car compared to the diesel car!

While this example gives spectacular differences (and electric cars do not suit all situations) there are tax savings to be made by carefully selecting a company car.

Another issue to be considered regarding company cars is that the assessable benefit of private fuel is the same regardless of the actual cost. Where the use of private fuel is low or moderate it may be cheaper for the employee to pay for their own fuel than pay the tax on the benefit of free fuel.

The availability of exempt benefits is another area that may be utilised if the employer agrees. For example, interest free loans of £10,000 or less are tax free, as are childcare vouchers of up to £55 per week for basic rate taxpayers. Employer contributions into pension schemes are also exempt from tax.

One way that some employers and employees can save tax (and sometimes NIC) is to enter into '**salary sacrifice**' arrangements with employees. This involves an alteration to the contract of employment so that the employee receives less pay in exchange for the provision of an agreed (often tax exempt) benefit.

example

A basic rate employee could enter into an agreement to 'sacrifice' £2,860 of salary (equivalent to £55 per week), in exchange for the same value of childcare vouchers. The employee could save £2,860 x 20% = £572 income tax, plus £2,860 x 12% = £343.20 primary NIC. The employer could also reduce secondary NIC by £2,860 x 13.8%.

Salary sacrifice schemes are widely used in some industries for a range of benefits. The Government is currently considering future legislation to restrict the use of such schemes.

marginal tax rates

For any tax minimisation plan to be wholly effective it is important to be aware of the marginal rate of tax of the individual concerned. This is the highest tax rate that they pay, and is usually the rate at which tax will be saved first. For example, saving tax on general or savings income for a higher rate taxpayer will be at 40% of the income, whereas only 20% for a basic rate taxpayer.

If an individual can avoid moving into the next tax band that will sometimes make the greatest saving. The impact of the different maximum amounts of personal savings allowance has already been noted, and this can add further importance to avoiding moving into higher bands.

For those with income just above the £100,000 level, the restriction on the personal allowance should also be considered when tax planning, since this effectively increases the marginal tax rate to 60%. Reducing adjusted net income by £1,000 would reduce tax by £600.

We saw earlier in this chapter that personal pension payments and gift-aid payments will provide tax relief at the marginal tax rate. Such payments will often provide effective ways of reducing tax liabilities.

married couples and civil partners

Where one spouse or civil partner has a different marginal tax rate to the other, then there is scope for the couple to save tax, particularly on savings or investments. There are no tax implications under Capital Gains Tax or Inheritance Tax when assets (including money or shares) are transferred between these individuals. Therefore if it was arranged that the person with the lower rate of tax owned money in a savings account or company shares, the income generated would attract less tax for the couple. The personal savings allowance and dividend allowance should also be taken account of when sharing assets.

Where the ownership of assets in a marriage or civil partnership is being considered, tax is not the only issue, and transfer of assets should only be contemplated when the full implications are understood by both parties. Where assets are held in joint names the income arising will be split equally.

Chapter Summary

■ The income tax computation is used to bring together income from various sources and calculate the tax. We have studied in some detail income from property, income from savings and investments, together with income from employment. We only need to have an outline understanding of profits from self-employment or partnership (trading income).

■ Income tax is calculated by working up through the bands, looking at general income, followed by savings income, and finally dividend income. Each of these classifications of income use their own tax rates.

■ Payments to charities under the gift aid scheme, and to pension providers for personal pension plan contributions are made net, which provides tax relief at basic rate. Further tax relief is provided for higher and additional rate taxpayers by increasing the basic rate tax band by the gross amounts of these types of payment.

■ Individuals with income over £100,000 are subject to the restriction or elimination of their personal allowance.

■ Tax planning can be used ethically to minimise tax by careful timing of some transactions, use of allowances and tax free income, and selections of benefits in kind. The individual's marginal tax rate can be used to inform relevant decisions.

Key Terms

Gift Aid
a scheme whereby individuals can make payment(s) to charities as net amounts, and the charity can claim the income tax back; higher rate taxpayers get further relief through their tax computations

personal pension plan
a type of pension plan (including a stakeholder pension) arranged for an individual – basic rate tax relief is provided by making payments net of 20% income tax while higher rate and additional rate taxpayers get further relief through their tax computations

salary sacrifice scheme
the alteration to the contract of employment so that the employee receives less pay in exchange for the provision of an agreed (often tax exempt) benefit

Activities

5.1   Jo paid £2,000 (net) under the gift aid scheme and £3,040 (net) to her pension provider as personal pension plan contributions. Her total taxable pay is £50,000 (all general income).

Calculate:

(a)   The gross equivalent of each payment.

(b)   The effective cost to her of each payment, after taking into account higher rate tax relief.

5.2   Matt has the following assessable income for the tax year:

Rental Income	£9,400
Employment Income	£26,500 (tax paid under PAYE £3,100)
Gross Interest Received	£5,000
Dividends	£12,000

He paid £2,400 (net) to a personal pension plan during the tax year.

Required:

Using an income tax computation, calculate the income tax liability and the amount of tax that is outstanding.

5.3   John has the following income in 2016/17:

• Employment income	£42,900
• Interest from ISAs	£1,020
• Bank account interest	£630
• Dividends	£3,500

Jon paid £300 (net) under gift aid.

Calculate John's adjusted net income and state the amount of personal savings allowance that he will be entitled to.

5.4   Mike received rent from furnished property in the tax year of £6,300. He paid out insurance of £350 in relation to the property, and spent £700 replacing a carpet. He has £250 of losses against property income carried forward from the previous year.

Mike is employed as an accountant, at a gross salary of £148,500 per year. He paid £53,000 under PAYE.

Mike uses his own car for occasional company business trips. During the tax year he travelled 2,000 business miles, and was reimbursed by his employer at 80p per mile. Mike paid his membership fees of £221 to the ACCA.

Mike has various investments, and during the tax year he received £1,400 in dividends from UK companies, plus £1,000 interest from his bank accounts.

Required:

(a) Calculate the assessable property income.

(b) Calculate the assessable employment income.

(c) Using an income tax computation, calculate the total tax liability for 2016/17, and the amount that has yet to be paid.

5.5 During the tax year, Rachel had employment income of £110,000 and received dividends of £6,000.

Required:

Calculate her total income tax liability (ie before deduction of tax paid) for the tax year, using the table given below.

	£
Employment income	
Dividends	
Personal allowance	
Taxable income	

5.6   Jim is a higher rate taxpayer with savings income in excess of the personal savings allowance. From the following list of separate possible actions, select those that will reduce his total Income Tax liability. You do not need to consider what impact the actions have on Jim's overall financial position.

Action	Select
(a) Withdraw savings from bank account and invest it in cash ISA	
(b) Change company car from petrol model to diesel model with same list price and CO_2 emissions	
(c) Make payments into personal pension plan	
(d) Borrow £8,000 interest free from employer and use proceeds to pay off personal credit card	
(e) Spend £1,000 replacing carpets in house that he rents to a tenant and generates profits	
(f) Donate money to charity through payroll giving scheme	

5.7   During the tax year, Robert had employment income of £109,000 and received dividends of £5,000. He paid £2,400 (net) into a personal pension scheme.

Calculate his total income tax liability (ie before deduction of tax paid), using the table given below.

	£
Employment Income	
Dividends	
Personal allowance	
Taxable income	

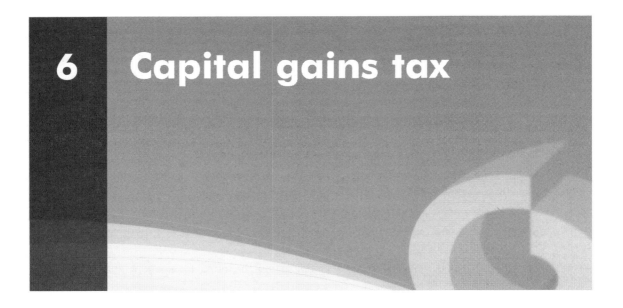

6 Capital gains tax

this chapter covers...

In this chapter we examine capital gains tax (CGT). This is a tax on the gains made on disposal on capital assets, and we will define a disposal, before examining which assets are chargeable and which are exempt.

We will then see how capital gains tax is calculated, by using the annual exemption and the appropriate rate of tax.

Next we look in detail at the calculations of each gain or loss, including the special rules that apply to spouses, civil partners and connected persons. In this section we learn what expenses can form allowable deductions in our calculations.

Losses and how they are relieved are examined next, and we will see how they are first set against the gains of the same tax year, before being carried forward if necessary.

We then learn how to calculate gains or losses when only part of an asset has been disposed of and the remaining part is kept. We use cost apportionment based on valuations at the date of sale to do this.

We then see how capital improvement (or 'enhancement') expenditure can form an allowable cost in the gains computation.

Next we examine the rather complicated rules surrounding principal private residence relief that apply when a property is not occupied throughout its ownership.

The final section deals with shares and the special rules relating to matching, pooling, and bonus and rights issues.

AN INTRODUCTION TO CAPITAL GAINS TAX

Capital Gains Tax (CGT) applies in certain circumstances to individuals who dispose of capital assets that they have previously acquired. It often applies to the sale or gift of an asset that may have been owned for quite some time. This can result in what is called a 'chargeable gain'. Note that CGT does not apply to trading assets, where items are regularly bought and sold to make a profit, as these are not classed as capital assets.

Although capital gains tax applies to both personal assets and business assets, we are only going to examine how it applies to personal assets in this book. Gains on the disposal of business assets are dealt with in the unit 'Business Tax' (see Osborne Books' *Business Tax*).

basis of assessment

Capital gains tax is applied to individuals by using the same tax years as those used for income tax. The basis of assessment for capital gains tax is the **chargeable gains less capital losses** arising from disposals that occur during the tax year.

We will look at how losses are dealt with later in this chapter. The main issues to understand at this point are that the tax is based on the total (or aggregate) of gains that have occurred, and that a gain can only arise when a **disposal** has taken place.

disposals

A disposal arises when an asset is:

- sold (or part of it is sold), or
- given away, or
- lost, or
- destroyed

Most of the situations that we will come across will be based on the sale or gift of an asset. You should remember, however, that a disposal can also result from loss or destruction of an asset. In the case of loss and destruction, the value of the asset is most likely to be assessed as zero, unless insurance proceeds are received.

Two special situations where disposals do not give rise to capital gains tax are:

- disposals arising because the owner has died, and
- any disposal between spouses (husband and wife) or civil partners

CHARGEABLE AND EXEMPT ASSETS

For capital gains tax to arise, the asset that has been disposed of must be a 'chargeable' asset. Exempt assets are entirely outside the CGT system. Instead of there being a long list of the assets that are chargeable, there is a fairly short list of assets that are exempt.

The simple rule is that if an asset is not exempt, then it must be chargeable!

A list of the main exempt assets is set out below:

exempt assets

- principal private residence – an individual's home (we will look at the rules for this later)
- cars
- wasting chattels (chattels are tangible, movable items; wasting means they have an estimated life of less than 50 years). Items of machinery for personal use (including, for example, clocks) are normally considered wasting chattels
- chattels bought and sold for £6,000 or less (there are also some special rules for those sold for more than £6,000 that we will look at later)
- Government Securities (Gilts)
- gifts made to charity
- shares that are held in an ISA

chargeable assets

Some typical personal assets that are chargeable and regularly feature in examination tasks include:

- antique furniture and paintings (since they have already lasted over 50 years)
- holiday homes
- land (eg a field not part of a main residence)
- shares

You must remember that these are only examples – all assets are chargeable unless they are exempt.

CALCULATION OF CAPITAL GAINS TAX

All individuals are entitled to an annual exempt amount – an **annual exemption** – for each tax year. This works in a similar way to a personal allowance under income tax. The exempt amount is deducted from the total net gains that have been calculated on the individual assets that have been disposed of during the year. Capital gains tax is then worked out on the balance.

The exempt amount is £11,100 in 2016/17. The exempt amount can only be used against capital gains (not set against income), and cannot be carried back or forward and used in another tax year.

Once the exempt amount has been deducted from the total net gains, the balance is subject to Capital Gains Tax. The rates of Capital Gains Tax are 10% and 20% for gains on all assets with the exception of those relating to disposals of residential property – these are taxed at 18% or 28%.

Although Capital Gains Tax is a separate tax from Income Tax, it uses the same band structure. Gains are treated as if they were added on top of taxable income, and the 10% (or 18%) rate is applied to gains falling within the basic rate band and the 20% (or 28%) rate applies to gains within the higher or additional rate bands.

The following diagram (which is an extended version of the one used earlier to illustrate income tax bands, and is not to scale) shows how the system works.

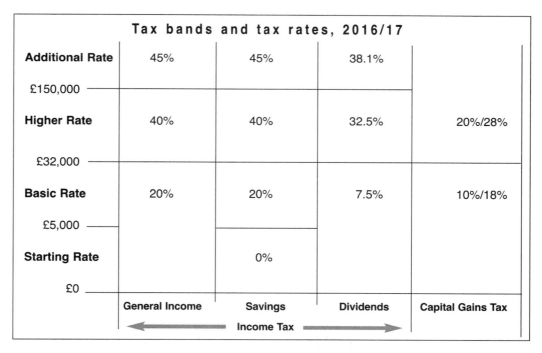

Although there are different rates for residential property gains and other gains, where a taxpayer has gains in both categories he / she can choose the most beneficial way to calculate the tax. We will examine this topic in more detail later in the chapter. At the moment we will concentrate on gains that do not derive from residential property.

If an individual is already a higher rate or additional rate taxpayer then any gains will be taxed at 20%. Where the taxpayer pays income tax only at the basic rate (or the starting rate) then gains will be taxed at 10% provided they do not exceed the basic rate band of £32,000 when added to taxable income. Where they do exceed this amount the excess will be taxed at 20%. The following example will illustrate the situation.

example

Rashid has total taxable general income of £30,000 after deducting his personal allowance. He made capital gains of £25,000 before deducting his exempt amount. The gains do not relate to residential property.

Rashid has taxable gains of £25,000 – £11,100 (exempt amount) = £13,900. He has £32,000 – £30,000 = £2,000 remaining in his basic rate band after accounting for his taxable income. Therefore £2,000 of his gains will be taxed at 10%, and the remainder taxed at 20%, as follows:

£2,000 x 10%	£200.00
£11,900 (the remainder of the £13,900) x 20%	£2,380.00
Total Capital Gains Tax	£2,580.00

We must now turn our attention to how to calculate the chargeable gain or loss on each separate disposal.

THE COMPUTATION OF EACH GAIN

Each disposal of a chargeable asset requires a calculation to determine the amount of any gain or loss. This computation follows a standard format that is in effect a mini income statement (profit & loss account) for the item disposed of. There are some minor variations to this format in particular circumstances, as we will see later. The basic format is as follows:

	£
Proceeds on disposal	X
less	
Incidental costs of disposal	(x)
Net proceeds	X
less	
Original cost	(x)
Incidental costs of acquisition	(x)
Gain (or loss)	X

proceeds on disposal

This normally refers to the amount that the asset realised when it was disposed of – ie the selling price. However there are some special situations where the figure used is different:

■ if the asset was given away (to anyone), or sold to a 'connected' person at less than the market value, the **market value** is used in the computation instead of the actual amount received. A chargeable gain can therefore arise even though the person disposing of the asset has received no proceeds

■ if the asset has been lost or destroyed then the asset will have been disposed of for zero proceeds, and zero will be used in the computation – and there could be a loss. The exception to this would be if an insurance claim has been made, in which case the amount of the claim proceeds would be used

transfer to spouse or civil partner

When an asset is transferred to a spouse or civil partner no capital gain arises, as mentioned earlier. This is achieved by treating the disposal proceeds as the amount needed to generate exactly zero gain or loss.

For example, if a wife had bought an asset some time ago for £10,000, (with no other costs) and gave it to her husband, the disposal proceeds would be treated as £10,000 so that no gain would arise. This would also mean that if the husband later sold the asset, his cost would also be considered to be £10,000, and any gain calculated on that basis.

A transfer between spouses or civil partners is often known as being made on a 'no gain, no loss' basis.

transfer to 'connected person'

As already noted, when an asset is sold to a connected person at less than market value, the market value is used in the computation of gains.

The following relatives of the person disposing of the asset are 'connected persons', and so are the relatives' spouses or civil partners:
■ ancestors and spouse's ancestors (parent, grandparent, etc)
■ siblings and spouse's siblings (brother, sister)
■ lineal descendants and spouse's lineal descendants (child, grandchild, etc)

So, for example the following people **would** each be a **connected person**, and any disposal would be deemed to be at market value:
■ brother's wife
■ wife's grandfather
■ daughter's husband

Each of the following people (for example) **would not** be a **connected person**:

- uncle or aunt
- cousin
- friend

Remember that **gifts** (whether to a connected person or not) are always deemed to be a disposal at market value, unless they are to a spouse or civil partner.

If a loss is incurred on a disposal to a connected person, the loss cannot be set against general gains, but can only be set against gains made on other disposals to the same person.

incidental costs of disposal

Incidental costs are the costs incurred by the taxpayer in selling the asset. Examples include advertising expenses, auction costs, or estate agent's fees for selling a property.

original cost, and incidental costs of acquisition

This relates to the amount paid to acquire the asset in the first place, plus any other costs incurred to buy it. Examples of these costs would include legal fees or auction costs. If the asset was given or bequeathed to the taxpayer, the market value at that time is used. We will examine in the next chapter how to deal with expenditure incurred later to improve the asset.

Case Study

HOLLY DAY:
COMPUTATION OF GAIN

Holly bought a cottage in Cornwall in August 1990 to use for her holidays. She paid £59,000 for the cottage, and also paid legal fees of £1,000 at the same time to arrange the purchase.

In the current tax year Holly sold the cottage for £240,000. The estate agent's fees for the sale were £3,000, and she incurred further legal fees of £2,000.

The cottage was Holly's only disposal of a chargeable asset during the tax year.

Holly is a higher rate income tax payer.

required

Calculate the gain on the disposal of the cottage, and the amount of Capital Gains Tax that Holly must pay.

solution

	£
Proceeds on disposal	240,000
less	
Incidental costs of disposal	(5,000)
Net proceeds	235,000

less	
Original cost	(59,000)
Incidental costs of acquisition	(1,000)
Gain	175,000

	£
Total gains for the tax year	175,000
Less exempt amount	(11,100)
Subject to CGT	163,900

Capital Gains Tax
£163,900 x 28% = £45,892

Holly pays CGT at 28% because she is already a higher rate taxpayer under Income Tax. As this is the disposal of a residential property the 20% rate does not apply.

DEALING WITH LOSSES

Capital losses arise from disposals in the same way as gains.

When losses have been calculated they are dealt with as follows:
- they are firstly set against gains arising in the same tax year, until these are reduced to zero, then
- any unused loss is carried forward to set against the next gains that arise in future tax years – at this stage the annual exempt amount can be safeguarded

We will now use an example to illustrate how this works.

example

Kulvinder has the following capital gains and losses, based on disposals occurring in 2014/15, 2015/16 and 2016/17.

	2014/15	2015/16	2016/17
	£	£	£
Gains	20,000	17,000	28,000
Losses	(35,000)		

For our calculations here, we will assume that the annual exempt amount remains at £11,100 for each of these three years.

required

Calculate how the loss can be used to offset the gains, and the amount subject to CGT each year.

2014/15

Because the loss of £35,000 occurred in the same year as the gain of £20,000, we must set off as much loss as possible against the gain, until the net gain is reduced to zero. There is no CGT liability this year. We then carry the loss balance of (£35,000 – £20,000 = £15,000) on to the next year.

2015/16

We now have a brought forward loss, and can offset it against the current gains. However because the loss is brought forward we only need to use up enough loss to bring the net gain down to the exempt amount.

We therefore use up £5,900 of the brought forward loss – just enough to bring the net gains for this year down to the exempt amount. There is no CGT liability in this year, and a loss of (£15,000 – £5,900 = £9,100) to carry forward.

2016/17

This year the remaining loss of £9,100 that has been brought forward is set against the gain of £28,000. From the balance of £18,900 is deducted the exempt amount of £11,100, leaving £7,800 that is subject to tax.

summary

	2014/15	2015/16	2016/17
	£	£	£
Losses working			
Loss brought forward	0	15,000	9,100
Loss incurred	35,000	0	0
Loss used up	20,000	5,900	9,100
Loss carried forward	15,000	9,100	0
Calculation of gains			
Gains	20,000	17,000	28,000
Loss set off	(20,000)	(5,900)	(9,100)
Net gains	0	11,100	18,900
Less exempt amount		(11,100)	(11,100)
Amount subject to CGT	0	0	7,800

Now apply what you have learnt about capital gains so far by working through the comprehensive Case Study that follows.

**Case
Study**

IVOR LOTT:
CAPITAL GAINS TAX PRINCIPLES

Ivor Lott made the following disposals during the tax year. Ivor has taxable income of £20,000 (after deducting his personal allowance).

- He sold his entire holding of 3,000 shares that he owned in Expo Limited for £6.75 each. He had bought all the shares in August 1998 for £10.00 each.

- He sold an antique table for £15,000 that he had bought in July 1996 for £7,000.

- He gave his daughter a field that was located 3 miles away from his home. He bought the field in April 1985 for £2,000. It was valued at £150,000 at the time of the gift, since it was now a possible development site.

- He sold his Jaguar E type car for £25,000. He had owned the car since January 1983 when he had bought it for £5,000.

required

- Calculate any gain or loss on each disposal.
- Calculate the capital gains tax payable by Ivor for the tax year (to the nearest £).

solution

Shares in Expo Limited

	£
Proceeds (3,000 x £6.75)	20,250
less cost (3,000 x £10)	(30,000)
Capital loss	(9,750)

Antique table

Proceeds	15,000
less cost	(7,000)
Gain	8,000

Field

Market Value	150,000
less cost	(2,000)
Gain	148,000

A gain arises even though Ivor received no proceeds.

Car

This asset is exempt from capital gains tax.

We can now add together the gains, and offset the loss.

	£
Gains:	
Antique table	8,000
Field	148,000
	156,000
less loss on shares	(9,750)
Net gains	146,250
less exempt amount	(11,100)
Subject to CGT	135,150

Capital Gains Tax

	£
£12,000* x 10%	1,200.00
£123,150 x 20%	24,630.00
£135,150	25,830.00

£32,000 – £20,000 taxable income

GAINS ON RESIDENTIAL PROPERTY AND OTHER ASSETS

We noted earlier that the tax rates for gains on residential property are 18% and 28%, whereas for all other capital gains they are 10% and 20%. Where an individual generates both types of gains in the same tax year the tax can be calculated in the way that is most beneficial.

The way that this is tackled is to offset against the gains on residential property as far as possible:

■ any capital losses incurred during the year, and then
■ the annual exempt amount

This will minimise the tax payable.

The following example will illustrate the calculation.

example

Julie has general taxable income of £25,000 (after deducting the personal allowance). During the year she incurred capital losses of £3,000, and generated capital gains of £30,000 on residential property and £22,000 on other assets.

The capital losses and annual exempt amount are set against the gains on residential property as follows:

	£
Residential property gain	30,000
Less capital losses	(3,000)
Less annual exempt amount	(11,100)
	15,900

Tax can then be calculated as follows:

	£
Residential property gains:	
£7,000 x 18% (to cumulative £32,000 including income)	1,260
£8,900 x 28% (the balance of £15,900)	2,492
Other gains:	
£22,000 x 20% (all at this rate)	4,400
Total capital gains tax	8,152

Note – provided the losses and annual exempt amount are offset against the gains on residential property, the tax will be minimised.

DEALING WITH PART DISPOSALS

We saw earlier that a disposal for Capital Gains Tax (CGT) purposes can relate to all or part of an asset. Although part disposal will not apply to many assets that are not divisible, it could apply (for example) to a piece of land.

If an asset was acquired as a whole, and then part of it is sold while the rest is retained, we need to compute the gain (or loss) on the part that was disposed of. The difficulty is that although we know how much the proceeds are for that part of the asset, we probably don't know how much of the original cost of the whole asset relates to that portion.

The way that this issue is tackled is to value the remaining part of the asset at the time of the part disposal. The original cost can then be apportioned by using these figures.

The cost applicable to the part disposed of is:

$$\text{Original cost of whole asset} \quad \times \quad \frac{A}{(A + B)}$$

where   A = Proceeds (or market value) of part disposed of, and

B = Market value of part retained

The following example will illustrate the calculation.

example

Heather bought a large field for £4,000 in January 1991 to keep her horses. In the current tax year she sold a part of the field for £3,000. At the same time the remainder of the field was valued at £9,000.

The portion of the original cost relating to the part of the field that was sold would be calculated as:

$$£4,000 \quad \times \quad \frac{£3,000}{(£3,000 + £9,000)}$$

This gives the cost as $£4,000 \times \frac{3,000}{12,000} = £1,000$.

The computation would then be carried out in the normal way:

	£
Proceeds	3,000
less cost (as calculated)	(1,000)
Gain	2,000

IMPROVEMENT EXPENDITURE

Where expenditure after acquisition is incurred to enhance an asset, and it is then disposed of in this improved condition, the improvement expenditure forms an allowable cost in the computation.

The expenditure must be of a 'capital' nature, and examples of this could include extending a building or having an antique professionally restored.

The following example illustrates the situation:

example

Sonny Daze bought a holiday cottage for £60,000 in September 1984. In January 1990 he spent £40,000 extending the property. He sold the cottage in the current tax year for £300,000.

	£
Proceeds	300,000
less original cost	(60,000)
improvement expenditure	(40,000)
Gain	200,000

PRINCIPAL PRIVATE RESIDENCES

We saw earlier in the chapter that a taxpayer's only or main residence – known as a principal private residence (PPR) – is exempt from Capital Gains Tax. Properties that have never been used as a main residence (for example holiday homes) are fully chargeable.

Where a taxpayer has two properties, and uses them both as main residences, only one can be treated as a PPR, and the taxpayer can elect as to which one it is. The election must be made to HMRC within two years of acquiring the second property. This could occur, for example, if a taxpayer used a property near his workplace during the week and another property situated elsewhere at weekends.

A property's status may change if it is occupied as a PPR for only part of its period of ownership. If this happens and the property is subsequently disposed of a gain can arise. In these circumstances the gain is worked out initially based on the whole period of ownership, and then apportioned to arrive at the exempt gain by multiplying the total gain by:

$$\frac{\text{period of occupation (as a PPR)}}{\text{period of ownership}}$$

Provided a property has been a PPR for some time during its ownership then the last 18 months of ownership are always regarded as part of the PPR occupation period. This is the case even if there is another PPR in use during that time.

We will now illustrate this using an example:

example

James bought a cottage in the Lake District for £50,000 on 1 January 1989 to use as a holiday home. He retired on 1 January 1999, and decided to sell his PPR and move into the cottage. On 1 January 2004 he bought a house in the Cotswolds as his PPR, moved there and went back to using the Lake District cottage as a holiday home.

On 1 January 2017 he sold the cottage in the Lake District for £250,000.

We first calculate the gain based on the whole period of ownership.

	£
Proceeds	250,000
less cost	(50,000)
Gain for whole period	200,000

We then time apportion the gain, counting the last 18 months of ownership as occupation, regardless of whether it actually was.

Owned: 1/1/89 - 1/1/17 = 28 years = 336 months

Actually occupied as PPR: 1/1/99 - 1/1/04 = 5 years = 60 months

Deemed occupation as PPR: 1/7/15 - 1/1/17 = 1½ years = 18 months

Total actual and deemed occupation = 78 months

Exempt gain: £200,000 x 78/336 = £46,429

Chargeable gain: £200,000 x 258/336 = £153,571

In addition to the above rule, there are other periods of absence that will count as being occupied as a PPR, provided:

■ the property was **actually occupied** as a PPR at some time both **before** and **after** the period, and

■ no other property is being treated as a PPR during the period of absence

These additional periods of 'deemed occupation' are:

■ three years in total for any reason,

■ up to four years when the taxpayer is absent due to UK employment,

■ any period when the taxpayer is living abroad due to employment

Case Study

LOVELY MOVER: PRINCIPAL PRIVATE RESIDENCE

Simon Lovely bought a house in London on 1 July 1991 for £50,000. He lived in it as his principal private residence (PPR) until 1 January 1999 when he started a new job in Scotland. He rented a flat in Edinburgh to live in, but he kept his London house. On 1 July 2008, he left his job in Scotland, and moved back into his London house. On 1 January 2010 he bought a house in Cornwall, which he elected to be his PPR and moved out of his London house. On 1 July 2016, he sold his London house for £510,000.

He made no other disposals in the tax year. Simon is a higher rate income tax payer.

required

• Calculate the chargeable gain on disposal of the London house.

• Calculate the capital gains tax payable by Simon for the year.

solution

	£
Sale proceeds	510,000
less cost	(50,000)
Gain before PPR relief	460,000

	Ownership (Years)	Actual/deemed occupation (Years)
Actual Occupation 1/7/91 - 1/1/99	7.5	7.5
Working in UK 1/1/99 - 1/7/08	9.5	7 *(see next page)
Actual Occupation 1/7/08 - 1/1/10	1.5	1.5
Absence 1/1/10 - 1/7/16	6.5	1.5 (last 1.5 years)
Total ownership	25	
Actual/deemed occupation		17.5

*The deemed occupation periods for 'working elsewhere in the UK' (4 years maximum) and 'absence for any reason' (3 years maximum) can both be claimed making a total of 7 years.

		£
Exempt gain	460,000 x 17.5/25 =	322,000
Chargeable gain	460,000 x 7.5/25 =	138,000

	£
Gain	138,000
Annual exemption	(11,100)
Amount subject to capital gains tax	126,900

Capital gains tax £126,900 x 28% = **£35,532.00**

Note that as this is a gain on a residential property it is charged at 28% not 20%.

SPECIAL RULES FOR CHATTELS

Chattels are tangible, moveable items such as furniture, jewellery, works of art and vehicles. As we saw in the last chapter, certain chattels are entirely exempt from Capital Gains Tax. These exempt chattels are:

■ wasting chattels (those with an expected life of less than 50 years)
■ cars
■ chattels that are both bought and sold for £6,000 or less

There are also some special rules about the amount of gain or loss that can occur when chargeable chattels are disposed of. Although these rules are not particularly complicated, they do need to be remembered.

chattels sold at a gain for over £6,000

In this situation the gain is limited to an amount of:

$$5/3 \text{ (Proceeds} - £6,000)$$

The 'proceeds' in this calculation is the gross proceeds – the amount received before deducting any selling expenses.

This is sometimes known as the 'chattel marginal relief'.

Suppose gains had been calculated on disposals as follows:

Disposal A

Proceeds	£9,000
Cost	£1,500
Gain	£7,500

The gain would be restricted to 5/3 (£9,000 – £6,000) = £5,000

£5,000 would therefore be used as the gain figure, since it is less than the £7,500 based on the normal calculation.

Disposal B

Proceeds	£9,000
Cost	£6,500
Gain	£2,500

Here the gain would also be restricted to £5,000, but since the calculated gain is only £2,500 the restriction would have no effect. The £2,500 gain would therefore stand.

chattels sold at a loss for less than £6,000

If the chattel had also been bought for less than £6,000 the transaction would be exempt from CGT. If the chattel had been acquired for over £6,000 then the loss would be limited by substituting £6,000 for the actual proceeds in the calculation.

For example, a chattel bought for £8,000 and sold for £3,000 would have a loss calculated as:

	£
Deemed proceeds	6,000
less actual cost	(8,000)
Loss	(2,000)

Make sure that you understand this process, and remember that it is the proceeds that are deemed to be £6,000. This is an area where it is easy to get confused if you are not careful.

We will now use a Case Study to help consolidate our understanding of the main issues that we have covered in this chapter so far.

Case Study

JUSTIN CREASE:
USING SPECIAL RULES

Justin made the following disposals. He is a higher rate income tax payer.

- He sold an antique lamp for £7,500. The lamp had cost £4,200 when he bought it in January 1999.

- He sold part of a large field for £10,000. He had bought the whole field in January 1990 for £8,000. At the time of the sale the market value of the remaining part of the field was £30,000.

- He sold a house in September 2016 for £325,000. He had bought the house in January 1999 for £160,000, and immediately used it as his main residence. He bought a new house in April 2015, and nominated that as his PPR. He rented out the original house from April 2015 until it was sold.

- He sold his gold cufflinks for £5,000. They had been left to him in his Uncle's will in September 1995. The value of the cufflinks at that time was £7,800.

- He bought an antique painting in January 1990 for £25,000. In September 1995 he paid £15,000 to have it professionally restored. The restored painting was sold for £90,000.

required

- Calculate the gain or loss on each applicable disposal.

- Calculate the amount of Capital Gains Tax that Justin will have to pay in respect of the tax year.

solution

Antique Lamp	£
Proceeds	7,500
less cost	(4,200)
Gain	3,300

but gain restricted to:

5/3 (£7,500 – £6,000) = £2,500

Field

Proceeds	10,000
less apportioned cost:	
£8,000 x £10,000 / (£10,000 + £30,000) (2,000)	
Gain	8,000

House

The house is entirely exempt. The period when it was rented out still counts as being occupied, as it is less than 18 months, and occurs at the end of the ownership period.

Cufflinks	£
Deemed proceeds	6,000
less value at acquisition	(7,800)
Loss	(1,800)

Antique painting	
Proceeds	90,000
less cost	(25,000)
improvement expenditure	(15,000)
Gain	50,000

We can now add together the gains, and set off the loss.

	£
Gains:	
Antique Lamp	2,500
Field	8,000
Antique painting	50,000
	60,500
less loss on cufflinks	(1,800)
Net gains	58,700
Less exempt amount	(11,100)
Subject to CGT	47,600

Capital Gains Tax
£47,600 x 20% = £9,520

MATCHING RULES FOR SHARES

We saw earlier that shares are chargeable assets, and that the computation for the acquisition and subsequent disposal of a block of shares is the same as for other assets.

The complication that can arise is when various quantities of the same type of share in the same company are bought and sold. The problem faced is similar to that in any stock valuation situation – how to determine which of the shares that were bought are deemed to be the same ones that were sold. The dilemma is solved in this situation by the application of strict **matching rules**.

When some shares are sold the matching process is carried out by working down the following categories of acquisition, skipping any that do not apply, until all the shares sold have been matched. A separate CGT computation is then used for each separate match.

1   Firstly, any shares bought on the **same day** that the disposal occurs are matched with that disposal.

2   Secondly, any shares bought in the **30 days after** the disposal are matched with those disposed of, (matching the earliest first if more than one acquisition). This probably seems illogical – selling something before it is bought!

3   Thirdly, any remaining shares not yet matched are deemed to have come from the 'FA 1985 pool' of shares. This is a device for merging shares.

The above order of matching is illustrated in the diagram below. The numbers in the diagram relate to the numbered stages described above.

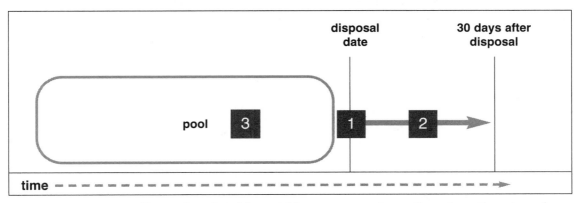

Remember that this matching process only applies where there have been several purchases of the same type of shares in the same company. It does not apply to a mixture of different companies shares, nor is it needed where a shareholding is bought and sold intact.

USING THE 'FA 1985 POOL'

This device was introduced in the 1985 Finance Act, and merges (or 'pools') shares in the same company and of the same type together. As we just saw, it occurs as the last of the matching rules, and is used to calculate the cost of shares acquired before the disposal date.

It is similar to the calculation of weighted average inventory valuations (as you have probably studied in Costing).

The pool needs to keep data relating to:

■ numbers of shares and

■ actual costs

These form the two main columns of the pool working.

The pool commences with the first shares bought. It then moves forward in time, adding each subsequent purchase of shares to provide cumulative numbers and costs of shares in the pool.

When any shares from the pool are disposed of, a proportion of the cumulative cost at the time of disposal is deducted from the pool, based on the numbers of shares. This cost amount that is deducted from the pool is then used in the gains calculation and compared with the proceeds in the normal way.

We will now demonstrate how the process works using a numerical example.

example

On 1/1/2017 Julie sold 10,000 ordinary shares in WyeCo Ltd for £10 each, from her shareholding of 25,000. Her shareholding had been built up as follows:

> 1/1/1988 bought 17,000 shares for £5.00 each
>
> 1/1/1993 bought 8,000 shares for £7.00 each

Since there are no acquisitions on or after 1/1/2017, the whole of the disposal of 10,000 shares will be matched with the pool. The pool will be built up as follows, with the disposal deducted as the latest transaction:

	Number	Cost
		£
1/1/1988 Purchase	17,000	85,000
1/1/1993 Purchase	8,000	56,000
Pool Totals	25,000	141,000
Less Disposal	(10,000)	(56,400)
Pool Balance after disposal	15,000	84,600

You should note the following:

- the cost figures for the disposal are a proportional amount of the pool costs before disposal, based on the number of shares (eg £141,000 x 10,000 / 25,000 = £56,400)

The computation for the disposal will now appear as follows:

	£
Proceeds (10,000 x £10)	100,000
Less cost	(56,400)
Gain	43,600

If at some future date there was another disposal of shares from the pool then the pool balance remaining (as on the previous page) would be used to determine the cost of the shares in the further disposal.

BONUS AND RIGHTS ISSUES

dealing with bonus shares

Bonus shares are additional shares given free to shareholders based on their current shareholding. This is sometimes called a 'scrip issue' and may be carried out as part of a capital restructuring of the company.

For CGT purposes the bonus shares are treated as if they were acquired at the same time as the original shares that generated the issue. For example a shareholder who owned 1,000 shares that were bought in January 2001 would be entitled to a further 200 shares if, later on, there were a bonus issue of 'one for five' shares. The total of 1,200 shares would be treated as bought in January 2001 for the amount paid for the 1,000 shares.

In virtually all situations, bonus shares are added to the pool when they are received. Since no payment is made, there is no adjustment to the cost figure.

If the bonus shares are received based on several acquisitions of original shares, the bonus shares will still be added into the pool, since the original shares will also be in the pool.

dealing with rights issues

A **rights issue** is the situation where additional shares are sold to existing shareholders, usually at a special price. For matching purposes, the shares that are bought in this way are treated as if they were bought with the original shares.

Rights issue shares will join the pool and be treated like any other share purchase. Their cost will be added into the pool.

We will now use a Case Study to make sure the principles relating to various matters studied are clear.

Case Study

CHER BYERS:
GAINS INCLUDING SHARES AND POOLING

Cher had acquired the following quoted ordinary shares in AbCo Plc (a listed company).

1/5/1985	1,000 shares at £4.00 each	£4,000
1/1/1990	Bonus issue of 1 for 4	
1/1/1992	1,750 shares at £4.20 each	£7,350
1/1/1995	1,500 shares at £4.10 each	£6,150 (Rights issue)
1/12/2001	1,800 shares at £5.10 each	£9,180

On 15/11/2001 she had sold 1,000 of her shareholding.

On 15/8/2016 she sold a further 2,500 ordinary shares in AbCo Plc for £10.00 each.

Cher also made the following disposals during 2016/17:

- she sold a plot of land for £20,000. This originally formed part of a larger field that she bought for £15,000 in January 1992. At the time of the sale the remaining portion of land was valued at £40,000

- she sold an antique ring for £6,600. She had bought it on 1 January 1999 for £3,500

- she sold an antique painting for £10,000. She had bought it in December 1996 for £14,000

Cher has taxable income of £29,000 (after deducting her personal allowance).

required

1   Identify which shares would have already been matched against the disposal that took place on 15/11/2001.

2   Show how the disposal of shares on 15/8/2016 will be matched against the acquisitions, and

3   Calculate the total gain arising from the sale of shares that took place on 15/8/2016.

4   Calculate any gains or losses arising from the disposal of the other assets.

5   Calculate the total Capital Gains Tax payable in respect of the tax year.

solution

1

The disposal of 1,000 shares on 15/11/2001 would have been matched with 1,000 of the 1,800 shares that were bought on 1/12/2001 for £5.10 each (shares bought in the 30 days after disposal). This leaves 800 of that purchase to join the pool.

2

Matching of the 15/8/2016 disposal of 2,500 shares will be entirely against the pool, since there were no shares of that type bought on that date or the following 30 days.

3

We will first need to build up the pool to August 2016, so that we can calculate the balances.

		Number	Cost
			£
1/5/1985	Purchase	1,000	4,000
1/1/1990	Bonus Issue	250	–
1/1/1992	Purchase	1,750	7,350
1/1/1995	Rights Issue	1,500	6,150
1/12/2001	Balance of Purchase (1,800 less 1,000 already matched)	800	4,080
		5,300	21,580
15/8/2016	Disposal	(2,500)	(10,179)*
	Pool balance after disposal	2,800	11,401

*The cost of the shares disposed of is calculated as:
(2,500 / 5,300) x £21,580 = £10,179

We can now calculate the gain on the disposal of shares, using the cost figure calculated in the pool.

	£
Proceeds	25,000
less cost	(10,179)
Gain	14,821

4

This task involves the computations on other asset disposals.

Land

	£
Proceeds	20,000
less apportioned cost:	
£15,000 x £20,000 / £60,000	(5,000)
Gain	15,000

Antique Ring

	£
Proceeds	6,600
less cost	(3,500)
Provisional gain	3,100

Gain is limited to 5/3 (£6,600 − £6,000) = £1,000

Antique Painting

	£
Proceeds	10,000
less cost	(14,000)
Loss	(4,000)

5

	£
Gains:	
Shares	14,821
Land	15,000
Antique ring	1,000
	30,821
Less loss on antique painting	(4,000)
Net gains	26,821
Less exempt amount	(11,100)
Subject to CGT	15,721
Capital Gains Tax	
£3,000 x 10%	300.00
£12,721 x 20%	2,544.20
	2,844.20

PAYMENT OF CAPITAL GAINS TAX

Capital Gains Tax is payable by individuals by the 31 January following the tax year in which the gains took place. It is payable at the same time (using a combined payment slip) as the balancing Income Tax payment for the same tax year. There is no system of payments on account for CGT. Capital Gains Tax for 2016/17 will therefore be paid on 31 January 2018.

Chapter Summary

- Capital gains tax is assessable on individuals who dispose of chargeable assets during the tax year. A disposal usually takes the form of the sale or gift of the asset. All assets are chargeable unless they are exempt. Exempt assets include principal private residences, cars, government securities (gilts), and certain chattels.

- Each disposal uses a separate computation that compares the proceeds or market value with the original cost of the asset.

- Losses are set off against gains. An annual exempt amount is deductible from the net gains. The balance is taxed at 10% or 20% depending on the individual's income, or 18% / 28% for gains on residential property.

- The cost of a part disposal is calculated by apportioning the cost of the whole asset. This is carried out by using the proceeds of the part disposed of as a proportion of the value of the whole asset at the time of disposal.

- Improvement expenditure that is reflected in the asset when disposed of is an allowable cost.

- Principal private residences are exempt assets provided they are occupied as such during the whole ownership. Certain periods of absence are treated as deemed periods of occupation. Where there are periods of absence that do not fall under these special rules, the exempt part of the gain on the property is calculated as a proportion of the whole gain, based on the period of occupation as a fraction of the period of ownership.

- Chattels that are acquired and sold for under £6,000 are exempt. Where they are sold at a gain for over £6,000 the gain is restricted to 5/3 of the gross proceeds minus £6,000. Where sold at a loss for under £6,000, the loss is restricted by substituting £6,000 for the actual proceeds in the computation.

- When shares of the same type in the same company are bought and sold at different times, matching rules are used to identify the shares disposed of. Firstly, shares bought on the day of disposal are matched. Secondly, those bought in the 30 days after disposal are matched. Thirdly, any earlier acquisitions are pooled and matched. This is known as the FA 1985 pool.

- Bonus and rights issues are treated as acquired at the time of the shares that they are derived from for matching purposes. They normally appear as part of the FA 1985 pool.

- Capital Gains Tax is payable by 31 January following the end of the tax year.

Key Terms		
	Capital Gains Tax (CGT)	a tax that applies to individuals who dispose of chargeable assets – it is charged at 18% or 28%
	disposal	a disposal for CGT purposes is the sale, gift, loss or destruction of an asset
	chargeable asset	this term is used to describe assets whose disposal can result in a CGT liability – all assets are chargeable unless they are exempt
	exempt asset	an asset that is not chargeable to CGT: exempt assets include principal private residences, cars, gilts, and some chattels
	chattel	a tangible, movable asset – ie the majority of personal possessions
	wasting chattel	a chattel with an expected life of fewer than 50 years
	annual exempt amount	the amount (also known as the 'annual exemption') that is deductible from an individual's net gains in a tax year before CGT is payable – the amount is £11,100 in 2016/17
	net proceeds	the proceeds from the sale of an asset, less any incidental costs of selling the asset
	capital loss	a capital loss results when the allowable costs of an asset exceed the sale proceeds (or market value). A loss is used by setting it against a gain in the same year, or if this is not possible, by carrying the loss forward to set against gains in the next available tax year
	connected person	normally a close relative; sales to a connected person at less than market value are deemed to be at market value
	part disposal	occurs when part of an asset is disposed of, but the remainder is retained
	improvement expenditure	capital expenditure that enhances an asset – if the enhancement is still evident at disposal, then the improvement expenditure is an allowable cost
	deemed occupation	periods of absence from a Principal Private Residence that are treated as periods of occupation for CGT purposes

chattels	tangible, moveable assets
wasting chattels	chattels with an expected life of less than fifty years
matching rules for shares	rules which determine which acquisitions of shares are identified with each disposal
bonus shares	extra shares given to shareholders in proportion to their current shareholding
rights issue	shares sold to existing shareholders at a special preferential price

Activities

6.1 Analyse the following list of assets into those that are chargeable to CGT and those that are exempt.

		Chargeable	Exempt
(a)	An antique painting sold for £10,000		
(b)	An individual's second home, used for weekends away		
(c)	Shares in CIC plc		
(d)	An individual's only home		
(e)	A small yacht		
(f)	An antique bed, bought for £500, and sold for £2,000		
(g)	A car		
(h)	Government securities		

6.2 Josie had a capital gain on her only disposal in the tax year of £15,000. It was not a gain on residential property. Her taxable income is £22,000.

Calculate the amount of Josie's Capital Gains Tax liability for the tax year.

6.3 Tariq had a capital gain on one disposal in the tax year of £35,000, and on the only other disposal, a capital loss of £9,000 Neither disposals were on residential property. His taxable income is £28,000 (after deducting personal allowance).

Calculate the amount of Tariq's Capital Gains Tax liability for the tax year.

6.4 April bought a holiday cottage in May 1995 for £60,000 and sold it in the current tax year for £130,000. She had no other disposals in the current tax year. April is a higher rate income tax payer.

Calculate April's CGT liability for the tax year.

6.5 Cliff bought a holiday flat in August 1998 for £50,000 and sold it in January 2017 for £165,000. In the same month he sold some shares for £32,000 which he had bought in July 2004 for £52,000. Cliff has taxable income of £35,000.

Calculate Cliff's CGT liability for the tax year.

6.6   Ivan Asset has capital losses brought forward from the previous tax year of £15,000. He made the following disposals during the tax year.

He sold his entire holding of 5,000 shares that he owned in Astro plc for £12.00 each. He had bought all the shares in June 1998 for £8.00 each.

He sold his Morgan car for £15,000. He had owned the car since January 1999 when he had bought it for £29,000.

He sold an antique dresser for £14,000 that he had bought in July 1996 for £9,000.

He gave his son 4,000 shares in Expo Ltd. He bought all the shares in January 1995 for £2.00 each. The shares were valued at £5 each at the time of the gift.

Ivan is a higher rate income tax payer.

Required:

(a)   Calculate any gain or loss arising from each of the disposals.

(b)   Calculate the amount of Capital Gains Tax payable for the tax year.

6.7   Justin Shaw has capital losses brought forward from the previous tax year of £18,000. He made the following disposals during the tax year. Justin's taxable income is £25,000:

He sold his yacht for £12,000. He had owned it since January 2001 when he had bought it for £23,000.

He sold his entire holding of 1,000 shares that he owned in Captain plc for £15.00 each. He had bought all the shares in June 1997 for £9.00 each.

He sold an antique painting of a ship for £14,000 that he had bought in July 1984 for £10,000.

He gave his daughter 3,000 shares in Boater Ltd. He bought all the shares in January 1996 for £3.00 each. The shares were valued at £7 each at the time of the gift.

Required:

(a)   Calculate any gain or loss arising from each of the disposals.

(b)   Calculate the amount of Capital Gains Tax payable for the tax year.

6.8 For each statement, tick the appropriate box.

		Actual proceeds used	Deemed proceeds used	No gain or loss basis
(a)	Grandfather gives an asset to his granddaughter			
(b)	Wife gives an asset to her husband			
(c)	Steve sells an asset to his friend for £13,000 when the market value is £16,000			
(d)	Mary sells an asset to her son's wife for £20,000 when the market value is £60,000			
(e)	Sue gives an asset to her civil partner, April			

6.9 **(1)** Andrew bought an asset in January 2000 for £26,000, selling it in December 2016 for £45,000. He paid auctioneers commission of 3% when he bought the asset and 5% when he sold the asset.

The gain on this asset is:

(a)	£20,470	
(b)	£15,970	
(c)	£17,530	
(d)	£19,000	

(2) True or false: advertising costs are not an allowable deduction as they are revenue expenses.

6.10 State which of the following statements are true:

(1) The annual exemption is applied before capital losses are deducted.

(2) Excess capital losses cannot normally be set against other taxable income.

(3) Capital gains are taxed at 20% for basic rate tax payers.

6.11 Alice made the following disposals in the tax year. She is a higher rate income tax payer.

She sold part of a piece of land for £30,000 that she had bought in January 1992. The whole piece of land had cost her £50,000 at that time. At the time of the sale the remaining land was valued at £120,000.

She sold her holiday cottage for £300,000 that she had bought for £60,000 in September 1985. She had also spent £50,000 in January 1992 extending the cottage.

Required:

Calculate the total capital gains tax for Alice for the tax year.

6.12 Bertie made the following disposals in the tax year. Bertie's taxable income is £20,000.

He sold an antique painting for £20,000 that he had bought for £5,000 in January 1992. He had the painting professionally restored in January 1995, and this cost £6,000.

He sold an antique table for £7,800. The table had been bought in January 1990 for £1,400.

Selling costs were £100.

Required:

Calculate the total capital gains tax for Bertie for the tax year.

6.13 Christine made the following disposals in the tax year.

She gave her sister an antique necklace that she had bought for £5,000. The necklace was valued at £8,000 at the time of the gift.

She sold her Jaguar E type car for £18,000. She had bought the car for £6,000, and spent £10,000 having it professionally restored.

On 31/12/2016 she sold her house in Dorking for £470,000. The house had been bought for £80,000 on 1/1/1989. Her use of the house was as follows:

1/1/1989 - 31/12/1998	occupied as Christine's PPR
1/1/1999 - 31/12/2000	rented out as Christine went on a world holiday
1/1/2001 - 31/12/2009	occupied as Christine's PPR
1/1/2010 - 31/12/2016	rented out as Christine moved to a new PPR.

Christine's taxable income is £30,000.

Required:

Calculate the total capital gains tax for Christine for the tax year.

6.14 David made the following disposals in the tax year. He is a higher rate income tax payer.

He sold 14,400 of his ordinary shares in Zydeco Ltd on 30/07/2016 for £72,000 in total. His shareholding in this company had been built up as follows:

1/1/1992   Bought 3,000 shares for £3.00 each.

1/1/1999   Bought 12,000 shares for £3.50 each.

1/1/2000   Bought rights issue shares on the basis of 1 for 5 at the price of £2.00 each.

David sold an antique dresser for £6,900. The dresser was bought for £3,000 in January 2000.

Required:

Calculate any gain made on:

- the disposal of shares in July 2016, and

- the disposal of the dresser

Calculate the amount of any CGT that will be payable.

6.15 Edward is a higher rate income tax payer. Edward had acquired the following quoted ordinary shares in Exray Plc (a listed company):

1/5/1985	1,000 shares	£ 8,000
1/1/1992	1,750 shares	£15,750
1/1/1995	1,500 shares	£10,650 (Rights issue)
1/12/2001	1,800 shares	£18,360

On 15/11/2001 he sold 2,000 of his shareholding.

On 15/7/2016 he sold a further 2,500 ordinary shares in Exray Plc for £12.00 each.

Edward also made the following disposals during the tax year:

- he sold a plot of land for £20,000. This originally formed part of a larger field that he bought for £5,000 in January 1988. At the date of disposal the remaining portion of land was valued at £80,000

- he sold an antique brooch for £9,600. He had bought it on 1 January 1999 for £5,500

- he sold an antique table for £12,000. He had bought it on 1 December 1999 for £13,500

Required:

(1) Identify which shares would have already been matched against the disposal that took place on 15/11/2001.

(2) Show how the disposal of shares on 15/7/2016 will be matched against the acquisitions, and

(3) Calculate the total gain arising from the sale of shares that took place on 15/7/2016.

(4) Calculate any gains or losses arising from the disposal of the other assets.

(5) Calculate the total Capital Gains Tax payable in respect of the tax year.

6.16 Robert bought a house on 1 February 2001 for £70,000. He lived in the house until 31 January 2006 when he moved in with his elderly parents. The house remained unoccupied until he sold it on 1 July 2016 for £205,000. This house is Robert's only property.

(a) Which periods are treated as occupied and which are not?

Occupation / Deemed Occupation	Non-occupation

(b) What is the chargeable gain on the property?

6.17 The following table relates to sales of chattels

Match the statements shown below to the correct asset details.

Asset	Sale proceeds	Cost	Statement
1	£4,000	£3,000	
2	£12,000	£8,000	
3	£7,000	£5,000	
4	£3,000	£8,000	
5	£15,000	£21,000	

Statements:

Exempt asset

Calculate gain as normal

Calculate loss as normal

Sale proceeds to be £6,000

Chattel marginal relief applies

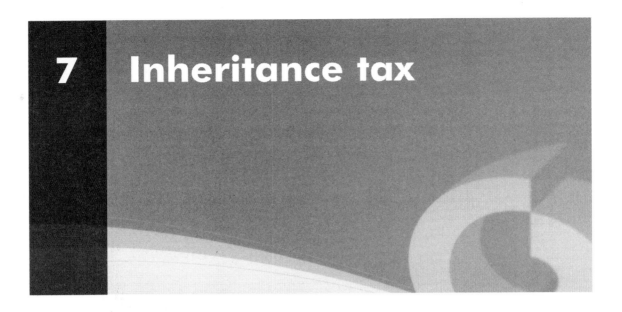

7 Inheritance tax

this chapter covers...

In this chapter we will examine the basic features of the rather complex topic of Inheritance Tax, which can apply to an individual's estate (net assets) left at death, and to some lifetime gifts.

We will start by explaining the various types of transfer and their implications. We will then see how an individual's estate can be charged to Inheritance Tax after they have died.

Next we will study lifetime transfers; gifts that are exempt, those that are chargeable, and those that are potentially exempt. Potentially exempt transfers will become exempt if the individual lives for at least seven years after making the transfer. We will see how all these types of transfers can affect Inheritance Tax.

We complete the chapter by looking at the special rules that can be applied at death relating to taper relief and gifts to charity.

OVERVIEW

Inheritance Tax (or IHT) can apply to the 'estate' of an individual who has died, and can also sometimes apply to gifts that an individual makes during their lifetime. Both these are known as 'transfers' – either transfers on death or lifetime transfers.

impact of domicile

Individuals who are UK domiciled (see Chapter 1) are subject to Inheritance Tax on property anywhere in the world. Non UK domiciled individuals are chargeable to Inheritance Tax only on property within the UK. Notice that there is a broad similarity between these rules and the ones we discussed earlier for income and gains. In certain circumstances individuals that are not UK domiciled can elect to be treated for Inheritance Tax purposes as if they were UK domiciled.

types of transfer

We need to understand the different types of 'transfer' for inheritance tax purposes, and what the implications are, as follows:

- **exempt transfers** – these are not chargeable to Inheritance Tax and can be excluded from any calculations. Some types of exempt transfers only relate to lifetime transfers, whilst others could be made either during the lifetime or at death.

- **chargeable lifetime transfers** – these transfers are subject to Inheritance Tax as soon as they are carried out. Those that exceed the cumulative tax threshold (or 'nil rate band') of £325,000 will involve payment of inheritance tax. We will see exactly how the tax threshold works shortly. The main category of chargeable lifetime transfers are transfers into specific trusts.

- **potentially exempt transfers** – these are lifetime transfers that will be exempt from Inheritance Tax if the donor (the individual making the gift) lives for at least 7 years after the gift is made. All lifetime transfers except exempt transfers and chargeable lifetime transfers are potentially exempt transfers – sometimes known as PETs.

- **transfers on death** – when an individual dies their 'estate' is made up of the assets that they owned minus any liabilities and funeral expenses. On death the individual is treated as making a final transfer of the whole of his or her estate.

TRANSFERS ON DEATH

We will start our explanation of how Inheritance Tax works by looking just at transfers made on death. Later on we can see how previous lifetime transfers by the same individual can affect the amount of inheritance tax.

There is a tax threshold of £325,000. **If there were no lifetime transfers**, the inheritance tax at death is normally calculated as follows:

- calculate the value of the estate

- deduct any exempt transfers

- deduct the tax threshold of £325,000

- calculate inheritance tax at **40%** on any balance.

The payment of Inheritance Tax relating to death is the responsibility of the **executor** of the individual's will (if there is a will), or the **administrator** of the estate if there is no will. An executor is a person (there can be more than one) that is named in the will with responsibility for dealing with the estate. In order to pay the inheritance tax, the executor or administrator will use money from the estate before it is distributed to the beneficiaries.

exempt transfers on death

The following are the main transfers made on death that are exempt from Inheritance Tax. The transfers are usually made because they are bequests stated in the individual's will.

- transfers to a UK domiciled **spouse** (husband or wife) or **civil partner**

- transfers to **charities**, **museums**, **universities** or **amateur sports clubs**

- transfers to qualifying **political parties**

- transfers of **land** to **housing associations**

Case Study

JOHN ABEL:
INHERITANCE TAX ON DEATH

situation

John Abel died, leaving an estate valued at £1,000,000. He had made no lifetime transfers. In his will he left £600,000 to his wife, Susan, £5,000 to charity, and the balance of his estate to be divided equally between his two children, William and Mary. The executor of the will was John's brother, Nigel.

required

- Calculate the amount of Inheritance Tax payable
- Calculate the amount to be received by William and Mary
- State who is responsible for paying the Inheritance Tax

solution

Calculation of Inheritance Tax:

	£
Total value of estate	1,000,000
Less exempt transfers:	
to Susan (spouse)	(600,000)
to charity	(5,000)
	395,000
Less nil rate band	(325,000)
	70,000
Inheritance Tax 40% of £70,000	28,000

Calculation of amount to be received by William and Mary:

	£
Total value of estate	1,000,000
Less transfers to Susan and to charity	(605,000)
Less Inheritance Tax	(28,000)
Balance of estate to be shared	367,000

William and Mary will receive £183,500 each.

The executor of the estate, Nigel, will be responsible for paying the Inheritance Tax, but the money will come from the estate. The Inheritance Tax will effectively reduce the value of the estate and hence the amount received by William and Mary.

transfer of unused threshold

Where an individual dies and the £325,000 nil rate band (or part of it) is not used, the individual's spouse or civil partner can subsequently add the unused part to their own nil rate band.

example

If Jill died and left all her estate to her husband John, none of the £325,000 nil rate band would have been used – since transfers to a spouse are exempt. When John died later on, Jill's unused nil rate band (the whole £325,000) would be added to his normal nil rate band, so his estate could be up to £650,000 before any Inheritance Tax was due.

LIFETIME TRANSFERS

As noted earlier, lifetime transfers may be exempt, chargeable, or potentially exempt. We will start by looking at the lifetime transfers that are exempt from Inheritance Tax.

exempt transfers

All the exempt transfers on death are also exempt if made as gifts during the individual's lifetime (see page 7.2):

- transfers to a UK domiciled **spouse** (husband or wife) or **civil partner**

- transfers to **charities**, **museums**, **universities** or **amateur sports clubs**

- transfers to **qualifying political parties**

- transfers of **land** to **housing associations**

In addition, the following transfers are exempt when made during the lifetime:

- up to **£3,000** worth of gifts given away each tax year. This is known as the annual exemption. Any unused part of the annual exemption can be carried forward – but only for one tax year, and is used after the annual exemption for that later year

- small gifts are exempt up to **£250 per person in a tax year**. This exemption cannot be carried forward or transferred, or used in conjunction with another exempt transfer

- **marriage gifts** are exempt, up to the following amounts:

  - £5,000 given by a parent

  - £2,500 given by a grandparent

  - £2,500 given by one of the individuals getting married

  - £1,000 by anyone else

- **regular gifts out of income**, without affecting normal lifestyle of the giver

- **payments to help with living costs of**

  - ex-spouse or civil partner

  - dependent relative who is old, ill or disabled

  - a child

example

Rachel made no gifts in the last tax year, but in the current tax year she gave the following:

*   £2,900 to her son, David when he got married
*   £150 to each of six grandchildren on their birthdays
*   £6,000 to her daughter, Ella to help her with a house deposit

The gifts to David and the six grandchildren would all be exempt under the marriage and small gifts exemptions. The current year and previous year annual exemption can both be set against the gift to Ella, making all £6,000 exempt.

chargeable lifetime transfers

Where a chargeable lifetime transfer is made (for example to certain trusts), Inheritance Tax will become immediately due if it (together with any other chargeable transfers in the last seven years) exceeds the £325,000 nil rate band. The annual allowances (where available) are deducted before checking whether the nil rate band is exceeded. The tax rate applied to the excess is 20%, and is paid by the recipient of the transfer (for example on behalf of the trust).

If the chargeable transfers (including those in the previous seven years) are less than £325,000 then no Inheritance tax will be due straight away, but part (or all) of the nil rate band will be used up. That means if the individual dies within the next seven years there will be less nil rate band to set against their estate.

example

Kelly made a transfer to a trust of £400,000 that was classed as a chargeable lifetime transfer. Kelly had made no other lifetime transfers. She could deduct two £3,000 annual exemptions, leaving a chargeable transfer of £394,000. The trust would pay Inheritance Tax of (£394,000 – £325,000) x 20% = £13,800.

If the individual who made the transfer subsequently dies within 7 years of the date of the transfer, their nil rate band will be reduced or eliminated by the chargeable transfer. At death, the tax on the chargeable transfer would also be re-calculated at the 40% rate, so that the receiver of the transfer would need to pay any additional tax due.

example

To continue the earlier example, if Kelly died two years after making the transfer, Inheritance Tax would be re-calculated on the transfer at 40% instead of the 20% already paid. This additional tax of £13,800 would be borne by the trust that received the transfer. This calculation is (£394,000 – £325,000) x 40%, minus £13,800 already paid.

The chargeable lifetime transfer was within 7 years of her death, and it used up all her nil rate band. If Kelly's estate at death was valued at £500,000 (after deducting any exempt transfers), Inheritance Tax of £500,000 x 40% = £200,000 would be payable from the estate.

potentially exempt transfers (PETs)

Lifetime transfers that are neither exempt nor chargeable are potentially exempt transfers. There is no immediate charge to Inheritance Tax when a potentially exempt transfer is made. If the individual who made that transfer lives for **at least 7 years after the date of the transfer**, there is **no** impact on Inheritance Tax at all. The **potentially** exempt transfer will have become **exempt**.

When an individual has died, any potentially exempt transfers that he or she made in the previous 7 years will be counted in the Inheritance Tax calculation. These transfers will therefore use up some (or all) of the nil rate band, and could become subject to Inheritance tax at 40%. If the PET exceeds the cumulative nil rate band the recipient is liable for the IHT. The calculation is carried out in chronological order, with the estate making up the final transfer.

example

Suppose Brian gave £50,000 to his daughter to help her buy her first house. If he had made no other transfers in the current or previous tax year he could deduct two £3,000 annual exemptions from the gift, leaving a potentially exempt transfer of £44,000. No Inheritance tax would be due at this point.

If Brian died two years later, leaving an estate valued at £350,000 (with no exempt transfers), the Inheritance Tax would be calculated as follows:

	£
Potentially exempt transfer – now chargeable	44,000
Nil rate band	325,000
Nil rate band available against estate	281,000
Estate	350,000
Less nil rate band balance (as above)	281,000
Chargeable to tax	69,000
IHT 40% of £69,000	27,600

The IHT would all relate to the estate, since the gift to Brian's daughter would be set against the nil rate band before the estate.

We will now use a case study to see how all the types of transfer together impact on Inheritance Tax.

Case Study

JENNY RUSH:
LIFETIME AND DEATH TRANSFERS

situation

Jenny (who had not made any transfers the previous tax year) made the following lifetime transfers:

31 May 2015	£150,000 payment into a trust (a chargeable transfer)
30 June 2015	£60,000 to her son, Jonah to pay for his university fees
30 Sept 2015	£4,000 to her daughter, Isabel when she got married

On 31 December 2016, Jenny died and left an estate valued at £650,000. Jenny's will listed the following beneficiaries:

• £300,000 to be paid to her husband, Wilf

• £10,000 to be paid to charity

• The balance to be shared equally between Jonah and Isabel.

required

Calculate the:

• Inheritance Tax payable during Jenny's lifetime.

• Inheritance Tax payable on Jenny's death.

solution

Inheritance Tax payable during lifetime:

Two £3,000 annual exemptions can be set against the chargeable transfer of £150,000, leaving £144,000. As this is below the £325,000 threshold there is no Inheritance Tax to pay during Jenny's lifetime.

Inheritance Tax payable on death:

The lifetime gift to Jonah of £60,000 is a potentially exempt transfer that has become chargeable at death.

The lifetime gift to Isabel is exempt under the marriage gift rules.

The nil rate band available at death is calculated as:

	£
Original nil rate band	325,000
Less Chargeable Lifetime Transfer	(144,000)
Less PET now chargeable	(60,000)
Nil rate band available against estate	121,000

		£
Inheritance Tax at death:		
Estate at death		650,000
Less exempt transfers	to husband Wilf	(300,000)
	to charity	(10,000)
Less nil rate band available (calculated above)		(121,000)
Subject to Inheritance Tax		219,000
Inheritance Tax at 40%		87,600

TAPERING RELIEF

Where lifetime transfers have been made, and Inheritance Tax is subsequently due on these transfers at death, there can be a reduction in tax. If the lifetime transfer was made between three and seven years before death, the amount of Inheritance Tax due on death will be as follows:

Time between transfer and death	% of normal tax due
3 to 4 years	80%
4 to 5 years	60%
5 to 6 years	40%
6 to 7 years	20%

These rates will only apply where the lifetime transfers exceed the nil rate band of £325,000, resulting in IHT becoming payable on death.

example

The only lifetime transfer made by Rashid was a PET of £375,000 (after exemptions) made on 30 September 2012. If Rashid subsequently died on 15 October 2016 (between 4 and 5 years after the transfer), the Inheritance Tax due relating to the PET would be calculated as:

	£
PET now changeable	375,000
Less nil rate band	(325,000)
Chargeable to Inheritance Tax	50,000
Inheritance Tax £50,000 x 40% x **60%**	12,000

This IHT would be payable by the recipient of the PET.

His estate would then all be charged at the normal rate of 40% (with no reduction). The nil rate band would have been used up.

GIFTS AT DEATH TO CHARITY

As already stated, gifts to charities in lifetime or on death are exempt. In addition, if 10% or more of the 'net value' of an estate is given to charity, then the normal rate of 40% Inheritance Tax can be reduced to 36%. The net value is calculated after deducting the nil rate band and other exempt transfers (for example to a spouse).

example

Sophie died and left a total estate of £900,000. Of this £200,000 was left to her civil partner, and £40,000 to charity.

The net estate would equal £900,000 – £200,000 – £325,000 = £375,000.

10% would equal 37,500. Since the gift to charity of £40,000 was more than this, the Inheritance Tax would be calculated at 36%, not 40%. IHT would be calculated as (£375,000 – £40,000 = £335,000) x 36% = £120,600.

PAYMENT OF INHERITANCE TAX

The normal due dates of payment are as follows:

■ for chargeable lifetime transfers made between 6 April and 30 September the IHT is payable by 30 April in the following year

■ for chargeable lifetime transfers made between 1 October and 5 April the IHT is payable six months after the end of the month in which the transfer was made

■ for transfers on death (including additional tax due on chargeable lifetime transfers and tax on PETs that have become chargeable) the tax is payable six months after the end of the month in which death occurred

Chapter Summary

■ Inheritance Tax is charged on death estates and some lifetime transfers that exceed a cumulative nil rate band (or threshold) of £325,000.

■ For Inheritance Tax purposes there are several types of transfer; exempt transfers, chargeable lifetime transfers, potentially exempt transfers, and transfers on death.

■ The only lifetime transfers that incur Inheritance Tax immediately are Chargeable Lifetime Transfers that (together with any in the previous seven years) exceed the £325,000 nil rate band.

■ Potentially exempt transfers (PETs) are lifetime transfers which are not exempt or chargeable. If the donor survives seven years after the gift these transfers become exempt. If the donor does not survive seven years these transfers are accounted for at death. The recipient is then liable for any IHT on the PET where it exceeds the cumulative nil rate band.

■ Unused nil rate band amounts can be passed on to a spouse or civil partner.

■ Tax at death on potentially exempt transfers now chargeable and chargeable lifetime transfers can be reduced if they occurred between three and seven years before death.

■ Gifts to charity at death can reduce the tax rate if the gifts exceed 10% of the net estate.

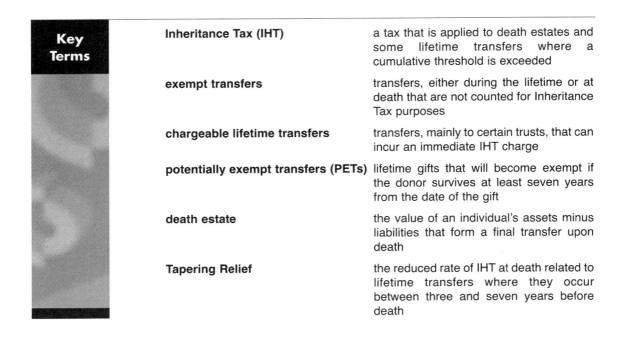

Key Terms	Inheritance Tax (IHT)	a tax that is applied to death estates and some lifetime transfers where a cumulative threshold is exceeded
	exempt transfers	transfers, either during the lifetime or at death that are not counted for Inheritance Tax purposes
	chargeable lifetime transfers	transfers, mainly to certain trusts, that can incur an immediate IHT charge
	potentially exempt transfers (PETs)	lifetime gifts that will become exempt if the donor survives at least seven years from the date of the gift
	death estate	the value of an individual's assets minus liabilities that form a final transfer upon death
	Tapering Relief	the reduced rate of IHT at death related to lifetime transfers where they occur between three and seven years before death

Activities

7.1 Theo died, leaving an estate of £595,000. He had not made any lifetime transfers. In his will he left the following:

£200,000 to his wife, Sophie.

£2,000 to his local amateur football club.

The balance of his estate to his daughter, Jane.

Calculate the Inheritance Tax due on the estate, and how much Jane will receive.

7.2 Angela and Tony had been married for many years, when Tony died. Tony had not made any lifetime transfers. In Tony's will he left £20,000 to each of their three adult sons, and the balance to Angela. Tony's estate was valued at £300,000.

Two years after Tony's death, Angela died. She had not made any lifetime transfers. Her estate was valued at £600,000, which was to be divided equally between her three sons.

Calculate the Inheritance Tax (if any) due on Angela's estate.

7.3 Examine the following list of transfers and identify which are only exempt for lifetime transfers, and which are exempt for both lifetime and death transfers.

Exempt Transfers	Only for Lifetime Transfers	Lifetime or Death Transfers
(a) Gifts of up to £3,000 in total		
(b) Transfers to spouse		
(c) Gifts to museums		
(d) Gifts to individuals of up to £250		
(e) Gifts to charities		
(f) Gifts to qualifying political parties		

7.4 Vikram made the following gifts during the current tax year. He had already used up the previous year's annual exemption.

- £500 into a savings account for his 10 year old niece, Amy. He had made similar transfers from his income each year since she was born.
- £200 to each of his six grandchildren.
- A ring worth £5,000 was given to his wife.
- A gift of £2,500 was made to a friend who was in financial difficulties.
- A gift costing £800 was given to a friend's daughter when she got married.
- Sports equipment costing £1,200 was given to the local amateur cricket club.

For each gift, state whether it will be exempt, and if so state the relevant exemption rule.

7.5 Mervyn (who had not made any transfers in recent tax years) made the following lifetime transfers:

31 January 2015   £220,000 payment into a trust (a chargeable transfer)

30 April 2015   £25,000 to his daughter, Josie.

30 June 2015   £25,000 to his daughter, June on her 21st birthday.

On 31 October 2016, Mervyn died and left an estate valued at £720,000. Mervyn's will listed the following beneficiaries:

- £325,000 to be paid to his wife, Julie
- £8,000 to be given to a qualifying political party

The balance to be shared equally between Josie and June.

Required:

Calculate the:

- Inheritance Tax payable during Mervyn's lifetime.
- Inheritance Tax payable on Mervyn's death.

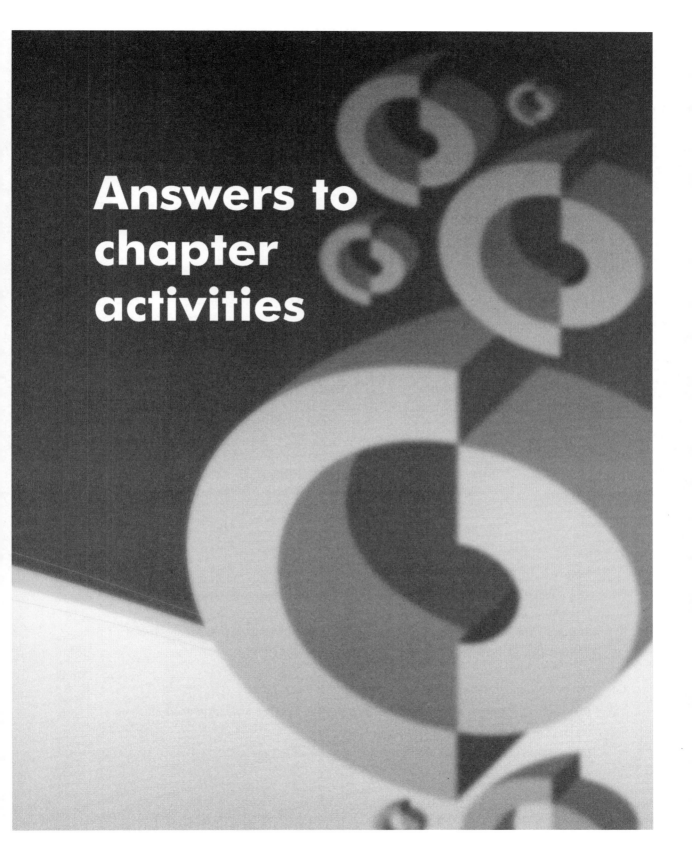

Answers to chapter activities

CHAPTER 1: INTRODUCTION TO TAXATION

1.1 **(a)**, **(c)** and **(f)** are false; **(b)**, **(d)** and **(e)** are true.

1.2 The following statements are true: **(a)**, **(e)**, **(f)**. The other statements are false.

1.3 Income Tax Computation for Mary

	£	£
		Tax Paid
Trading Income	2,800	–
Employment Income	12,300	260
Property Income	4,500	–
Total Income	19,600	260
Less Personal Allowance	11,000	
Taxable Income	8,600	
Income Tax Calculation:		
£8,600 x 20%	1,720.00	
Income Tax Liability	1,720.00	
Less already paid	260.00	
Income tax to pay	1,460.00	

Note:

The trading income is based on the accounting year to 30/9/16, because it ends in the tax year 2016/17.

The employment income is based on the amount received in the tax year, irrespective of the period that it relates to.

1.4 **(a)** Dividend Income, part of Savings and Investment Income

(b) Employment Income – full title Employment, Pensions and Social Security Income

(c) Exempt

(d) Savings Income, part of Savings and Investment Income

(e) Exempt

(f) Property Income

1.5   Income Tax Computation for John

	£	£
		Tax Paid
Employment Income	10,800	0
Property Income	3,000	–
Total Income	13,800	0
Less Personal Allowance	11,000	
Taxable Income	2,800	

Income Tax Calculation:

	£
£2,800 x 20%	560.00
Income Tax Liability	560.00
Less already paid	0.00
Income tax to pay	560.00

Note:

The property income includes the March rent since it operates on an accruals basis.

The interest on an ISA is exempt.

1.6   Income Tax Computation for Megan

	£	£
		Tax Paid
Trading Income	14,700	–
Employment Income	34,400	4,680
Total Income	49,100	4,680
Less Personal Allowance	11,000	
Taxable Income	38,100	

Income Tax Calculation:

		£
£32,000 x 20%		6,400.00
£6,100 x 40%		2,440.00
£38,100	Income Tax Liability	8,840.00
	Less already paid	4,680.00
	Income tax to pay	4,160.00

Note:

The trading income is based on the accounting year to 31/12/16, because it ends in the tax year 2016/17.

The employment income is based on the amount received in the tax year, irrespective of the period that it relates to.

1.7   **(a)**, **(b)** and **(d)** are true; **(c)**, **(e)** and **(f)** are false.

CHAPTER 2: INCOME FROM PROPERTY

2.1

		£
Rental Income for period 6/7/16 - 5/4/17	(£5,000 x 9/12)	3,750
Less		
Insurance (9 months at £25)		225
Replacement of fridge		200
Assessable property income for 2016/17		3,325

2.2

		£
Rental Income for period 6/11/16 - 5/4/17	(£400 x 5)	2,000
Less		
Mortgage Interest (5 months at £150)		750
Insurance (5 months at £30)		150
Agent's Fees (£1,200 x 5/12)		500
Assessable property income for 2016/17		600

The legal fees relating to the purchase of the property are a capital cost.

2.3

	£	£
Rental Income Receivable		10,000
less allowable expenditure:		
Council Tax	700	
Water Rates	300	
Insurance	400	
Replacement of carpets	2,500	
Managing Agent's Charges	1,000	
		4,900
Assessable property income		5,100

2.4

	No 1	No 2	No 3	Total
	£	£	£	£
Rental Income	8,000	6,000	5,500	19,500
Less allowable expenditure:				
Council Tax	800	650	400	1,850
Loan Interest	3,600	2,000	4,000	9,600
Property Insurance	400	300	250	950
Redecoration	–	600	–	600
Repainting Windows	500	450	500	1,450
Other Repairs	300	400	200	900
Accountancy Fees	150	150	150	450
Profit / (Loss)	2,250	1,450	0	3,700
Less loss brought forward				1,000
Property Income				2,700

The council tax for property three is allowed since it relates to the period that it is occupied. Other expenses for this property relate to the period that it was owned for the business of letting and are therefore allowable. The purchase of furniture was not replacement items, and is therefore not allowable.

2.5 (1) Property Income Computation

	£	£
Rental Income Receivable		11,500
less allowable expenditure:		
Accountancy Fees	400	
Council Tax	650	
Water Rates	350	
Insurance	300	
Replacement furniture	2,000	
Mortgage Interest	2,300	
Managing Agent's Charges	1,000	
		7,000
Property Income		4,500

(2)   Income Tax Computation

	Income	Tax Paid
	£	£
Employment Income	41,500	6,100
Property Income	4,500	–
Total Income	46,000	6,100
Less Personal Allowance	11,000	
Taxable Income	35,000	

Income Tax Calculation:

32,000 x 20%		6,400.00
3,000 x 40%		1,200.00
35,000	Income Tax Liability	7,600.00
	Less Paid	6,100.00
	Income Tax to Pay	1,500.00

2.6

	Three bedroom house	**One bedroom flat**
	£	£
Income	8,100	4,500
Expenses:		
Irrecoverable rent*	1,800	
Management charge	504	
Council tax and water		1,400
Insurance		270
Profits	5,796	2,830

*Irrecoverable rent could alternatively be shown by reducing the income figure.

CHAPTER 3: INCOME FROM SAVINGS AND INVESTMENTS

3.1   (e) £Nil

The personal allowance of £11,000 covers the employment income of £10,000 and the first £1,000 of the savings income. The next £5,000 of savings income falls into the starting rate for savings income and is charged at 0%. The remaining £500 of savings income is covered by the personal savings allowance (of up to £1,000) so is also taxed at 0%.

3.2   **(a)**   **Savings Income:**

£1,300
£1,000 (personal savings allowance)
£300 x 20% = £60.00 tax on savings income

(b)   **Dividend income**

£1,600
£1,600 (dividend allowance)
Nil   No tax due on dividends

3.3   **Income Tax Computation**

	Income	Tax Paid
	£	£
Employment Income	28,500	3,500
Property Income	1,900	–
B/S Int	1,500	–
Dividends	4,000	–
Total Income	35,900	3,500
Less Personal Allowance	11,000	
Taxable Income	24,900	

Analysis of Taxable Income:

General Income	(£28,500 + £1,900 – £11,000)	£19,400
Savings Income		£1,500
Dividend Income		£4,000
		£24,900

Income Tax Calculation:	£	£
General Income:		
£19,400 x 20%	3,880.00	
		3,880.00
Savings Income:		
£1,000 x 0% (personal savings allowance)	0.00	
£500 x 20%	100.00	
£1,500		100.00
Dividend Income:		
£4,000 x 0% (dividend allowance)	0.00	
		0.00
Income Tax Liability		3,980.00
Less Paid		3,500.00
Income Tax to Pay		480.00

3.4   Income Tax Computation

	Income	Tax Paid
	£	£
Employment Income	14,400	680
Savings Income	2,000	–
Dividend Income	5,500	–
Total Income	21,900	680
Less Personal Allowance	11,000	
Taxable Income	10,900	

Analysis of Taxable Income:

General Income	(£14,400 – £11,000)	£3,400
Savings Income		£2,000
Dividend Income		£5,500
		£10,900

Income Tax Calculation:

General Income:		
£3,400 x 20%	680.00	
		680.00
Savings Income:		
£1,600 x 0% (starting rate)	0.00	
£400 x 0% (personal savings allowance)	0.00	
£2,000		
		0.00
Dividend Income:		
£5,000 x 0% (dividend allowance)	0.00	
£500 x 7.5%	37.50	
		37.50
Income Tax Liability		717.50
Less Paid		680.00
Income Tax to pay		37.50

3.5 **(a)**

Savings Income

Date	Details	Assessable Amount
		£
30/6/16	3.5% War Loan	1,500.00
31/1/17	Bank of North'd	11,875.00
31/3/17	Osborne Bank	750.00
Total		14,125.00

Dividend Income

Date	Details	Assessable Amount
		£
31/5/16	Growth plc	4,000.00

Note that the interest from the ISA is exempt, and that the receipts dated 31/3/16 and 30/6/17 fall outside the tax year 2016/17.

(b)

Income Tax Computation

	Income £	Tax paid £
Employment Income	5,000	0
Savings Income (as above)	14,125	0
Dividend Income (as above)	4,000	0
Total Income	23,125	0
Less Personal Allowance	11,000	
Taxable Income	12,125	

Analysis of Taxable Income:

General Income	(£5,000 – £11,000 = £–6,000)	£NIL
Savings Income	(£14,125 – £6,000)	£8,125
Dividend Income		£4,000
		£12,125

Note that the balance of the personal allowance is set against savings income.

Income Tax Calculation:

General Income – NIL

Savings Income:

£5,000 x 0% (starting rate)	0.00	0.00
£1,000 x 0% (personal savings allowance)	0.00	
£2,125 x 20%	425.00	
£8,125		425.00

Dividend Income:

£4,000 x 0% (dividend allowance)	0.00	
		0.00
Income Tax Liability		425.00

3.6 (a) Cash ISAs and stocks and shares ISAs are subject to a maximum total investment in the tax year of £15,240, (d) ISAs can only be opened by individuals who are resident in the UK *and* (f) The total invested in a stocks and shares ISA can subsequently be transferred to a cash ISA

CHAPTER 4: INCOME FROM EMPLOYMENT

4.1

		£
Basic salary		18,000
Commission rec'd	30/4/16	1,200
	31/7/16	1,450
	31/10/16	1,080
	31/1/17	1,250
Employment income assessable amount 2016/17		22,980

4.2 Assessable **(b)**, **(c)**, **(e)**, **(f)**, **(g** – home to work is private mileage), **(h)**

Tax-Free **(a)**, **(d** – interest rate higher than official rate)

4.3

		£
Basic salary		20,000
Company car	(£11,500 x 21%)	2,415
Fuel for car	(£22,200 x 21%)	4,662
Credit card – private expenditure		100
(fuel covered by scale charge)		
Healthcare insurance		730
Employment income assessable amount		27,907

4.4

		£
Basic Salary		28,000
Less 6% pension contribution		1,680
Pay (per P60)		26,320
Vouchers (cost to employer)		850
Excess business mileage paid		
10,000 x (60p – 45p)	1,500	
1,500 x (60p – 25p)	525	
		2,025
		29,195
Less allowable expenses:		
Professional fees		(170)
Assessable amount		29,025

The hotel expenses received relate to an allowable cost, and so are exempt.

4.5

		£
(1)	Basic Salary	40,000
	Less 5% pension contribution	2,000
	Pay (per P60)	38,000
	Company car (1)	
	(£18,000 x 34% x 5/12)	2,550
	Company car (2)	
	((£20,000 − £1,000) x 25% x 7/12)	2,770
		5,320
	Car fuel (car 2 only)	
	(£22,200 x 25% x 7/12)	3,237
	Dental treatment	500
	Employment Income	47,057

(Mortgage is not assessable since interest charged is over official rate)

(2) **Income tax computation**

	Income	Tax paid
	£	£
Employment Income	47,057	6,000
Interest	1,500	–
Dividends	2,000	–
	50,577	6,000
less personal allowance	11,000	
	39,557	

Analysis of income:

General	£36,057
Savings	£1,500
Dividends	£2,000
Total	£39,557

Tax:	£	£
General Income:		
£32,000 x 20%	6,400.00	
£4,057 x 40%	1,622.80	
£36,057		8,022.80
Savings Income:		
£500 x 0% (Personal Savings Allowance)	0.00	
£1,000 x 40%	400.00	
£1,500		400.00
Dividend Income:		
£2,000 x 0% (Dividend Allowance)	0.00	
		0.00
Tax liability		8,422.80
Less Paid		6,000.00
Balance to be paid		2,422.80

4.6

Contract of service is for:	Employment
Contract for services is for:	Self Employment
Choose work hours and charge for work done	Self Employment
No need to provide own equipment	Employment
Told how, when and where to do work	Employment
Can employ helper or substitute	Self Employment
Correct substandard work at own cost	Self Employment

4.7 **(1)** (£24,000 + £20,000)/2 x 7/12 x 2.00% = £256 (rounded down)

(2) (c) 75,000

(3) (a) Yes, (b) Yes, (c) No

(4) (a) 5,600

(5) (a) and (d) are correct

4.8

	Nissan	Mitsubishi	Honda
Benefit % Applicable	7%	7%	26%
Benefit for Private Use of Car	£2,141	£2,326	£7,962
Benefit for Private Use of Fuel	£0	£1,554	£5,772
Total Assessable Benefit	£2,141	£3,880	£13,734
Annual Income Tax Cost	£856	£1,552	£5,493

4.9

	Primary Contributions £	Secondary Contributions £
George	141.36	162.01
Helen	360.66	479.41
Natasha	0.00	196.51
Vikram	355.86	446.29

CHAPTER 5: PREPARING INCOME TAX COMPUTATIONS

5.1 **(a)** Gross equivalent amounts:

Gift Aid £2,000 x 100/80 = £2,500

Pension £3,040 x 100/80 = £3,800

(b) Jo will get tax relief at her highest rate (40%) on her gross payments (20% when the payments are made and the other 20% in calculating her tax). The cost of her payments after tax relief will therefore be:

Gift Aid £2,500 less 40% = £1,500.

Pension £3,800 less 40% = £2,280.

5.2
Income Tax Computation

	£	£ Tax Paid
Property Income	9,400	–
Employment Income	26,500	3,100
Interest rec'd	5,000	–
Dividend income	12,000	–
Total Income	52,900	3,100
Less Personal Allowance	11,000	
Taxable Income	41,900	

Analysis of Taxable Income:

General Income (£9,400 + £26,500 − £11,000)	£24,900
Savings Income	£5,000
Dividend Income	£12,000
	£41,900

The basic rate band will be increased by the gross equivalent of the pension payment (£2,400 x 100/80 = £3,000). This makes the new top of the band £32,000 + £3,000 = £35,000.

Income Tax Calculation:

General Income:	£	£
£24,900 x 20%	4,980.00	
		4,980.00
Savings Income		
£500 x 0% (personal savings allowance)	0.00	
£4,500 x 20%	900.00	
£5,000		900.00
Dividend Income		
£5,000 x 0% (dividend allowance)	0.00	
£100 x 7.5% (to £35,000 cumulative)	7.50	
£6,900 x 32.5%	2,242.50	
£12,000		
		2,250.00
Income tax liability		8,130.00
Less paid		3,100.00
Balance to pay		5,030.00

5.3

Employment income	£42,900
Bank account interest	£630
Dividends	£3,500
Less:	
Personal savings allowance	£(630)
Dividend allowance	£(3,500)
Gift aid payments (gross)	£(375)
Adjusted net income	£42,525

Since the adjusted net income is below £43,000 John is a basic rate taxpayer, and his personal savings allowance could be up to £1,000. In this case it is £630.

5.4

(a)

	£
Rent received	6,300
less insurance	350
less replacement of carpet	700
	5,250
less loss b/f	250
Property income	5,000

(b)

	£
Salary	148,500
Excess mileage allowance paid 2,000 miles x (80p – 45p)	700
Less ACCA membership fee	(221)
Employment Income	148,979

(c)   Income Tax Computation

	£	£ Tax Paid
Property Income	5,000	nil
Employment Income	148,979	53,000
Savings and Investment Income:		
(interest rec'd)	1,000	–
(dividend income)	1,400	–
Total Income	156,379	53,000
Less Personal Allowance (eliminated)	0	
Taxable Income	156,379	

Analysis of Taxable Income:	
General Income (£5,000 + £148,979)	153,979
Savings Income	1,000
Dividend Income	1,400
	156,379

Income Tax Calculation:

General Income	£	£
£32,000 x 20%		6,400.00
£118,000 x 40%		47,200.00
£3,979 x 45%		1,790.55
£153,979		55,390.55
Savings Income		
£1,000 x 45% (no personal savings allowance)		450.00
Dividend Income £1,400 x 0% (dividend allowance)		0.00
Income tax liability		55,840.55
Less paid		53,000.00
Balance to pay		2,840.55

5.5

	£
Employment income	110,000
Dividends	6,000
	116,000
Personal allowance	5,500
Taxable income	110,500
General Income:	
£32,000 x 20%	6,400
£72,500 x 40%	29,000
Dividend Income	
£5,000 x 0%	0
£1,000 x 32.5%	325
Tax Liability	35,725

Workings:

Adjusted net income is £110,000 + £6,000 − £5,000 = £111,000

Personal allowance is £11,000 − 50% (£111,000 − £100,000) = £5,500.

5.6   (a), (c), (e) and (f) will reduce his total Income Tax liability.

5.7

	£
Employment income	109,000
Dividends	5,000
	114,000
Personal allowance	8,000
Taxable income	106,000
General Income:	
(£32,000 + £3,000) x 20%	7,000
(£101,000* − £35,000) x 40%	26,400
Dividend Income	
£5,000 x 0%	0
Tax Liability	33,400

Workings:

Adjusted net income: £109,000 + £5,000 − £3,000 − £5,000 = £106,000

Personal allowance: £11,000 − 50% x (£106,000 − £100,000) = £8,000

*General income: £109,000 − £8,000 = £101,000

CHAPTER 6: CAPITAL GAINS TAX

6.1   Chargeable Assets: **(a)**, **(b)**, **(c)**.

Exempt Assets: **(d)**, **(e** − wasting chattel**)**, **(f** − chattel sold for a gain for under £6,000**)**, **(g)**, **(h)**.

6.2

	£	£
Gain	15,000	
less annual exempt amount	(11,100)	
Amount subject to CGT	3,900	
Capital Gains Tax:		
£3,900 x 10% (all within basic rate band)		390.00

6.3

Capital Gain	35,000	
Less Capital Loss	(9,000)	
Net Gain	26,000	
less annual exempt amount	(11,100)	
Amount subject to CGT	14,900	
Capital Gains Tax:		
£4,000 x 10% (£32,000 – £28,000)		400.00
£10,900 x 20%		2,180.00
		2,580.00

6.4

Proceeds	130,000
less Cost	(60,000)
Gain	70,000

Gain	70,000
less Annual exempt amount	(11,100)
Subject to CGT	58,900

Capital Gains Tax (all at 28%)	16,492.00

6.5 **Flat**

	£
Proceeds	165,000
less Cost	(50,000)
Gain	115,000

Shares

Proceeds	32,000
less Cost	(52,000)
Loss	(20,000)

Gain on flat	115,000
Loss on shares	(20,000)
Net Gain	95,000

less Annual exempt amount	(11,100)
Subject to CGT at residential property rates	83,900

Capital Gains Tax	
£83,900 x 28%	23,492.00

6.6   Ivan Asset

(a)

Shares in Astro plc

	£
Proceeds (5,000 x £12.00)	60,000
less cost (5,000 x £8.00)	(40,000)
Gain	20,000

Morgan Car – Exempt Asset

Antique dresser

	£
Proceeds	14,000
less cost	(9,000)
Gain	5,000

Shares in Expo Ltd

	£
Market Value (4,000 x £5.00)	20,000
less cost (4,000 x £2.00)	(8,000)
Gain	12,000

(b)

The gains can now be added together, and the loss offset.

	£
Gains:	
Astro plc shares	20,000
Antique dresser	5,000
Expo Ltd shares	12,000
	37,000
less loss brought forward	(15,000)
	22,000
less annual exempt amount	(11,100)
Taxable amount	10,900
Capital gains tax £10,900 x 20%	2,180

6.7   Justin Shaw

(a)

Yacht – Exempt as a wasting chattel

Shares in Captain plc	£
Proceeds (1,000 x £15.00)	15,000
less cost (1,000 x £9.00)	(9,000)
Gain	6,000

Antique painting	£
Proceeds	14,000
less cost	(10,000)
Gain	4,000

Shares in Boater Ltd	£
Market Value (3,000 x £7.00)	21,000
less cost (3,000 x £3.00)	(9,000)
Gain	12,000

(b)

	£
Gains:	
Captain plc shares	6,000
Antique painting	4,000
Boater Ltd shares	12,000
	22,000
less loss brought forward*	(10,900)
Balance	11,100
less annual exempt amount	(11,100)
Taxable amount	0

There is no CGT liability.

*Of the £18,000 loss brought forward, only £10,900 is used so that a balance of £11,100 is left (the amount of the annual exemption). This leaves a loss of £7,100 to be carried forward to the next year.

6.8 **(a)** Deemed proceeds used
     (b) No gain or loss basis
     (c) Actual proceeds used
     (d) Deemed proceeds used
     (e) No gain or loss basis

6.9 **(1)** (b) £15,970
     (2) False

6.10 **(1)** False
      (2) True
      (3) False

6.11

	£
Land	
Proceeds	30,000
less apportioned cost:	
£50,000 x £30,000 / £150,000	(10,000)
Gain	20,000
Cottage	
Proceeds	300,000
less cost	(60,000)
extension	(50,000)
Gain	190,000
Total gains: Land	20,000
Cottage	190,000
Total gains	210,000
less annual exempt amount	(11,100)
Amount subject to CGT	198,900

Capital Gains Tax:

Residential property (£190,000 − £11,100) x 28%	£50,092.00
Other assets £20,000 x 20%	£4,000.00
	£54,092.00

6.12

	£
Painting	
Proceeds	20,000
less cost	(5,000)
less restoration	(6,000)
Gain	9,000

	£
Table	
Proceeds	7,800
less costs: (£1,400 + £100)	(1,500)
Provisional Gain	6,300

But gain limited to 5/3 (£7,800 − £6,000) = £3,000.

		£
Total gains:	Painting	9,000
	Table	3,000
		12,000
less annual exempt amount		(11,100)
Amount subject to CGT		900

Capital Gains Tax:

£900 x 10% = £90.00 (all in basic rate band)

6.13

Necklace	£
Deemed Proceeds (market value)	8,000
less cost:	(5,000)
Gain	3,000

Gain limited to 5/3 (£8,000 − £6,000) = £3,333 − limit does not apply.

Car is an exempt asset

House is not entirely exempt:

World holiday period counts as deemed occupation under the 'absence for any reason' rule since it is for less than 3 years and is between periods of actual occupation.

1½ of the final seven years of absence counts as deemed occupation since it was a PPR before this. The house is therefore exempt for 22.5 years of the 28 years ownership, and chargeable for 5.5 years.

	£
Proceeds	470,000
less cost	(80,000)
Gain	390,000
Exempt £390,000 x 22.5/28	313,393
Chargeable £390,000 x 5.5/28	76,607

Gains Summary:

	£
Necklace	3,000
House	76,607
Total Gains	79,607
less exempt amount	(11,100)
Taxable	68,507

Capital Gains Tax

Residential property (£76,607 – £11,100 = £65,507)

	£
£2,000 x 18%	360.00
£63,507 x 28%	17,781.96
Other assets	
£3,000 x 20%	600.00
	18,741.96

6.14 The 3,000 rights issue shares (1 for 5 of the total holding of 15,000 shares) acquired in January 2000 will be linked with the original shares from which the rights derive. Therefore the shares will be added into the pool.

The disposal of 14,400 shares in July 2016 will therefore be matched entirely with the shares that are in the pool:

Pool Working:

		Number	**Cost**
			£
1/1/1992	Purchase	3,000	9,000
1/1/1999	Purchase	12,000	42,000
		15,000	51,000
1/1/2000	Rights Issue (1 for 5)	3,000	6,000
		18,000	57,000
30/7/2016	Disposal	(14,400)	(45,600)
	Pool balance after disposal	3,600	11,400

Share disposal July 2016	£
Proceeds	72,000
less cost	(45,600)
Gain	26,400

Dresser disposal	
Proceeds	6,900
less cost	(3,000)
Gain	3,900

But gain limited to 5/3 (£6,900 – £6,000) = £1,500.

		£
Total gains:	Shares	26,400
	Dresser	1,500
Total gains		27,900
less annual exempt amount		(11,100)
Amount subject to CGT		16,800

Capital Gains Tax

£16,800 x 20%	3,360.00

6.15 **(1)** The 2,000 shares sold on 15/11/2001 would have been matched against:
- the 1,800 shares bought on 1/12/2001, and
- 200 shares from the FA 1985 pool

(2) The 2,500 shares sold on 15/7/2016 will be matched against the shares in the FA 1985 pool.

(3) *Pool Working:*

		Number	Cost £
1/5/1985	Purchase	1,000	8,000
1/1/1992	Purchase	1,750	15,750
1/1/1995	Purchase	1,500	10,650
		4,250	34,400
15/11/2001	Part Disposal	(200)	(1,619)
		4,050	32,781
15/7/2016	Disposal	(2,500)	(20,235)
	Pool balance	1,550	12,546

Disposal of Shares:

Proceeds (2,500 x £12)	30,000	
less cost	(20,235)	as above
Gain	9,765	

(4) Computations on other asset disposals:

Land

	£
Proceeds	20,000
less apportioned cost:	
£5,000 x £20,000 / £100,000	(1,000)
Gain	19,000

Antique Brooch

	£
Proceeds	9,600
less cost	(5,500)
Provisional gain	4,100

Gain is limited to 5/3 (£9,600 − £6,000) = £6,000 − limit does not apply.

Antique table

	£
Proceeds	12,000
less cost	(13,500)
Loss	(1,500)

(5)

	£
Gains:	
Shares	9,765
Land	19,000
Antique brooch	4,100
	32,865
less loss on antique table	(1,500)
Net gains	31,365
less annual exempt amount	(11,100)
Amount subject to CGT	20,265

Capital Gains Tax:
£20,265 x 20% = £4,053.00

6.16 (a)

Occupation / Deemed Occupation	Non-occupation
1/2/2001 - 31/1/2006	1/2/2006 – 31/12/2014
1/1/2015 - 1/7/2016	

(b)

Total gain calculation:	£
Proceeds	205,000
Cost	70,000
Total gain	135,000

Chargeable gain   £135,000 x $\dfrac{\text{non-occupation period}}{\text{total ownership period}}$

= £135,000 x $\dfrac{107 \text{ months}}{185 \text{ months}}$

= £78,081

6.17

Asset	Sale proceeds	Cost	Statement
1	£4,000	£3,000	Exempt asset
2	£12,000	£8,000	Calculate gain as normal
3	£7,000	£5,000	Chattel marginal relief applies
4	£3,000	£8,000	Sale proceeds to be £6,000
5	£15,000	£21,000	Calculate loss as normal

CHAPTER 7: INHERITANCE TAX

7.1

	£
Inheritance Tax calculation:	
Estate	595,000
Less exempt transfer to Sophie	(200,000)
Less exempt transfer to amateur football club	(2,000)
Less nil rate band	(325,000)
Amount subject to IHT	68,000
Inheritance Tax at 40%	27,200
Calculation of amount received by Jane:	
Estate	595,000
Less transfer to Sophie	(200,000)
Less transfer to amateur football club	(2,000)
Less Inheritance Tax	(27,200)
Balance due to Jane	365,800

7.2 Tony's unused nil rate band will be transferred to Angela. This unused band will be £325,000 – (£20,000 x 3) = £265,000. This is because the transfer on Tony's death to Angela is exempt.

The Inheritance Tax on Angela's death will be calculated as:

	£
Estate	600,000
Less nil rate band (£325,000 + £265,000)	(590,000)
Chargeable to IHT	10,000
Inheritance Tax at 40%	4,000

7.3 **(a)** and **(d)** are only for lifetime lransfers; the others are for lifetime or death transfers.

7.4 • £500 into a savings account for his 10 year old niece, Amy. This is exempt since it is classed as regular expenditure out of income.

• £200 to each of his six grandchildren. These are exempt as each individual receives less than £250 in the tax year.

• A ring worth £5,000 was given to his wife. This is exempt as a gift to his wife.

• A gift of £2,500 was made to a friend who was in financial difficulties. This will be exempt as it is the only gift that falls under the £3,000 annual exemption.

• A gift costing £800 was given to a friend's daughter when she got married. This is exempt, covered by the marriage gifts up to £1,000 by 'anyone else'.

• Sports equipment costing £1,200 was given to the local amateur cricket club. This is exempt, since all gifts to amateur sports clubs are exempt.

7.5 Inheritance Tax due in lifetime:

The chargeable transfer will not result in any IHT payable immediately, since (after deducting two £3,000 annual exemptions) it is £214,000, which is below the £325,000 threshold.

The gift to Josie is a PET of £25,000, less annual exemption of £3,000 = £22,000. The gift to June is a PET of £25,000.

Inheritance tax on death:

	£
Estate	720,000
Less exempt transfer to wife, Julie	(325,000)
Less exempt transfer to political party	(8,000)
Less nil rate band	
(£325,000 – £214,000 – £22,000 – £25,000)	(64,000)
Chargeable to IHT	323,000
Inheritance Tax at 40%	129,200

Reference Material

for AAT Assessment of Personal Tax

Finance Act 2016

Professional conduct in relation to taxation

For assessments from 1 January – 31 December 2017

Note: this reference material is accessible by candidates during their live computer based assessment for Personal Tax.

This material was current at the time this book was published, but may be subject to change. Readers are advised to check the AAT website or Osborne Books website for any updates.

Reference material for AAT assessment of Personal Tax

Introduction
This document comprises data that you may need to consult during your Personal Tax computer-based assessment. The material can be consulted during the sample and live assessments through pop-up windows. It is made available here so you can familiarise yourself with the content before the test.

Do not take a print of this document into the exam room with you. Unless you need a printed version as part of reasonable adjustments for particular needs, in which case you must discuss this with your tutor at least six weeks before the assessment date.

This document may be changed to reflect periodical updates in the computer-based assessment, so please check you have the most recent version while studying. This version is based on Finance Act 2016 and is for use in AAT assessments 1 January – 31 December 2017.

Contents

1. Interpretation and abbreviations

Context

Tax advisers operate in a complex business and financial environment. The increasing public focus on the role of taxation in wider society means a greater interest in the actions of tax advisers and their clients.

This guidance, written by the professional bodies for their members working in tax, sets out the hallmarks of a good tax adviser, and in particular the fundamental principles of behaviour that members are expected to follow.

Interpretation

1.1   In this guidance:
- 'Client' includes, where the context requires, 'former client'.
- 'Member' (and 'members') includes 'firm' or 'practice' and the staff thereof.
- For simplicity, 'she' and 'her' are used throughout but should be taken to include 'he' and 'his'.
- Words in the singular include the plural and words in the plural include the singular.

Abbreviations

1.2   The following abbreviations have been used:

CCAB	Consultative Committee of Accountancy Bodies
DOTAS	Disclosure of Tax Avoidance Schemes
GAAP	Generally Accepted Accounting Principles
GAAR	General Anti-Abuse Rule in Finance Act 2013
HMRC	Her Majesty's Revenue and Customs
MLRO	Money Laundering Reporting Officer
NCA	National Crime Agency (previously the Serious Organised Crime Agency, SOCA)
POTAS	Promoters of Tax Avoidance Schemes
SRN	Scheme Reference Number

2. Fundamental principles

Overview of the fundamental principles

2.1   Ethical behaviour in the tax profession is critical. The work carried out by a member needs to be trusted by society at large as well as by clients and other stakeholders. What a member does reflects not just on themselves but on the profession as a whole.

2.2   A member must comply with the following fundamental principles:

Integrity

To be straightforward and honest in all professional and business relationships.

Objectivity

To not allow bias, conflict of interest or undue influence of others to override professional or business judgements.

Professional competence and due care

To maintain professional knowledge and skill at the level required to ensure that a client or employer receives competent professional service based on current developments in practice, legislation and techniques and act diligently and in accordance with applicable technical and professional standards.

Confidentiality

To respect the confidentiality of information acquired as a result of professional and business relationships and, therefore, not disclose any such information to third parties without proper and specific authority, unless there is a legal or professional right or duty to disclose, nor use the information for the personal advantage of the member or third parties.

Professional behaviour

To comply with relevant laws and regulations and avoid any action that discredits the profession.

Each of these fundamental principles is discussed in more detail in the context of taxation services.

3. Tax returns

Definition of tax return (return)

3.1 For the purposes of this Chapter, the term 'return' includes any document or online submission of data that is prepared on behalf of the client for the purposes of disclosing to any taxing authority details that are to be used in the calculation of tax due by a client or a refund of tax due to the client or for other official purposes and, for example, includes:
- Self-assessment returns for income or corporation tax;
- VAT and Customs returns;
- PAYE returns;
- Inheritance tax returns;
- Returns or claims in respect of any other tax or duties where paid to the UK Government or any authority, such as a devolved government.

3.2 A letter giving details in respect of a return or as an amendment to a return including, for example, any voluntary disclosure of an error should be dealt with as if it was a return.

Taxpayer's responsibility

3.3 The taxpayer has primary responsibility to submit correct and complete returns to the best of her knowledge and belief. The return may include reasonable estimates where necessary. It follows that the final decision as to whether to disclose any issue is that of the client.

Member's responsibility

3.4 A member who prepares a return on behalf of a client is responsible to the client for the accuracy of the return based on the information provided.

3.5 In dealing with HMRC in relation to a client's tax affairs a member must bear in mind her duty of confidentiality to the client and that she is acting as the agent of her client. She has a duty to act in the best interests of her client.

3.6 A member must act in good faith in dealings with HMRC in accordance with the fundamental principle of integrity. In particular the member must take reasonable care and exercise appropriate professional scepticism when making statements or asserting facts on behalf of a client. Where acting as a tax agent, a member is not required to audit the figures in the books and records provided or verify information provided by a client or by a third party. A member should take care not to be associated with the presentation of facts she knows or believes to be incorrect or misleading nor to assert tax positions in a tax return which she considers have no sustainable basis.

3.7 When a member is communicating with HMRC, she should consider whether she needs to make it clear to what extent she is relying on information which has been supplied by the client or a third party.

Materiality

3.8 Whether an amount is to be regarded as material depends upon the facts and circumstances of each case.

3.9 The profits of a trade, profession, vocation or property business must be computed in accordance with GAAP subject to any adjustment required or authorised by law in computing profits for those purposes. This permits a trade, profession, vocation or property business to disregard non-material adjustments in computing its accounting profits. However, it should be noted that for certain small businesses an election may be made to use the cash basis instead.

3.10   The application of GAAP, and therefore materiality, does not extend beyond the accounting profits. Thus the accounting concept of materiality cannot be applied when completing tax returns (direct and indirect), for example when:
- computing adjustments required to accounting figures so as to arrive at taxable profits;
- allocating income, expenses and outgoings across the relevant boxes on a self-assessment tax return;
- collating the aggregate figures from all shareholdings and bank accounts for disclosure on tax returns.

Disclosure

3.11   If a client is unwilling to include in a tax return the minimum information required by law, the member should follow the guidance in Chapter 5 Irregularities. 3.12 - 3.18 give guidance on some of the more common areas of uncertainty over disclosure.

3.12   In general, it is likely to be in a client's own interests to ensure that factors relevant to her tax liability are adequately disclosed to HMRC because:
- her relationship with HMRC is more likely to be on a satisfactory footing if she can demonstrate good faith in her dealings with them; and
- she will reduce the risk of a discovery or further assessment and may reduce exposure to interest and penalties.

3.13   It may be advisable to consider fuller disclosure than is strictly necessary. The factors involved in making this decision include:
- the terms of the applicable law;
- the view taken by the member;
- the extent of any doubt that exists;
- the manner in which disclosure is to be made; and
- the size and gravity of the item in question.

3.14   When advocating fuller disclosure than is strictly necessary a member should ensure that her client is adequately aware of the issues involved and their potential implications. Fuller disclosure should not be made unless the client consents to the level of disclosure.

3.15   Cases will arise where there is doubt as to the correct treatment of an item of income or expenditure, or the computation of a gain or allowance. In such cases a member ought to consider carefully what disclosure, if any, might be necessary. For example, additional disclosure should be considered where:
- a return relies on a valuation;
- there is inherent doubt as to the correct treatment of an item, for example, expenditure on repairs which might be regarded as capital in whole or part, or the VAT liability of a particular transaction; or
- HMRC has published its interpretation or has indicated its practice on a point, but the client proposes to adopt a different view, whether or not supported by Counsel's opinion. The member should refer to the guidance on the Veltema case and 3.19.

3.16   A member who is uncertain whether her client should disclose a particular item or of its treatment should consider taking further advice before reaching a decision. She should use her best endeavours to ensure that the client understands the issues, implications and the proposed course of action. Such a decision may have to be justified at a later date, so the member's files should contain sufficient evidence to support the position taken, including contemporaneous notes of discussions with the client and/or with other advisers, copies of any second opinion obtained and the client's final decision. A failure to take reasonable care may result in HMRC imposing a penalty if an error is identified after an enquiry.

3.17   The 2012 case of Charlton clarified the law on discovery in relation to tax schemes disclosed to HMRC under DOTAS. The Upper Tribunal made clear that where the taxpayer has:
(i)   disclosed details of a significant allowable loss claim;
(ii) declared relatively modest income/ gains; and/or
(iii) included the SRN issued by HMRC on the appropriate self-assessment tax return,

an HMRC officer of reasonable knowledge and skill would be expected to infer that the taxpayer had entered into a tax avoidance scheme (and that fuller details of such scheme would be contained in the relevant AAG1 Form). As a result, HMRC would be precluded, in most cases, from raising a discovery assessment in a situation where the client implemented the disclosed scheme and HMRC failed to open an enquiry within the required time.

3.18   It is essential where a member is involved in the preparation of a self-assessment tax return which includes a scheme disclosed under DOTAS that the member takes care to ensure:
- that the tax return provides sufficient details of any transactions entered into (in case the AAG1 Form is incomplete);
- that the SRN is recorded properly in the appropriate box included for this purpose on a self-assessment tax return; and
- the SRN is shown for the self-assessment return for each year in which the scheme is expected to give the client a tax advantage.

Supporting documents

3.19   For the most part, HMRC does not consider that it is necessary for a taxpayer to provide supporting documentation in order to satisfy the taxpayer's overriding need to make a correct return. HMRC's view is that, where it is necessary for that purpose, explanatory information should be entered in the 'white space' provided on the return. However, HMRC does recognise that the taxpayer may wish to supply further details of a particular computation or transaction in order to minimise the risk of a discovery assessment being raised at a later time.

3.20   Further HMRC guidance says that sending attachments with a tax return is intended for those cases where the taxpayer 'feels it is crucial to provide additional information to support the return but for some reason cannot utilise the white space'.

Approval of tax returns

3.21   It is essential that the member advises the client to review her tax return before it is submitted.

3.22   The member should draw the client's attention to the responsibility which the client is taking in approving the return as correct and complete. Attention should be drawn to any judgemental areas or positions reflected in the return to ensure that the client is aware of these and their implications before she approves the return.

3.23   A member should obtain evidence of the client's approval of the return in electronic or non-electronic form.

4. Tax advice

Introduction

4.1   Giving tax advice covers a variety of activities. It can involve advising a client on a choice afforded to her by legislation, for example, whether to establish a business as a sole trader, partnership or company. It could be advising on the tax implications of buying or selling an asset or business, or advising on succession planning.

4.2   For the most part clients are seeking advice on how to structure their affairs, either personal or commercial, in a way that is tax efficient and ensures that they comply with their legal and regulatory requirements. Transactions based on advice which are centred around non-tax objectives are less likely to attract scrutiny or criticism from stakeholders and are much more likely to withstand challenge by HMRC.

4.3   Some tax strategies have been the subject of heated public debate, raising ethical challenges. Involvement in certain arrangements could subject the client and the member to significantly greater compliance requirements, scrutiny or investigation as well as criticism from the media, government and other stakeholders and difficulties in obtaining professional indemnity insurance cover.

4.4   The definition of 'avoidance' is an evolving area that can depend on the tax legislation, the intention of Parliament, interpretations in case law and the varying perceptions of different stakeholders and is discussed further below.

4.5   A member should consider the contents of this Chapter carefully when giving tax advice and the potential negative impact of her actions on the public perception of the integrity of the tax profession more generally.

4.6   Clearly a member must never be knowingly involved in tax evasion, although, of course, it is appropriate to act for a client who is rectifying their affairs.

Tax planning vs tax avoidance?

4.7   Despite attempts by courts over the years to elucidate tax 'avoidance' and to distinguish this from acceptable tax planning or mitigation, there is no widely accepted definition.

4.8   Publicly, the term 'avoidance' is used in the context of a wide range of activities, be it multinational structuring or entering contrived tax-motivated schemes. The application of one word to a range of activities and behaviours oversimplifies the concept and has led to confusion.

4.9   In a 2012 paper on tax avoidance, the Oxford University Centre for Business Taxation states that transactions generally do not fall into clear categories of tax avoidance, mitigation or planning. Similarly, it is often not clear whether something is acceptable or unacceptable. Instead the paper concludes that there is:
'a continuum from transactions that would not be effective to save tax under the law as it stands at present to tax planning that would be accepted by revenue authorities and courts without question.'

Member's responsibility in giving tax planning advice

4.10   A member is required to act with professional competence and due care within the scope of her engagement letter.

4.11   A member should understand her client's expectations around tax advice or tax planning, and ensure that engagement letters reflect the member's role and responsibilities, including limitations in or amendments to that role. The importance of this has been highlighted by the Mehjoo case.

4.12   A member does not have to advise on or recommend tax planning which she does not consider to be appropriate or otherwise does not align with her own business principles and ethics. However, in this situation the member may need to ensure that the advice she does not wish to give is outside the scope of her engagement. If the member may owe a legal duty of care to the client to advise in this area, the member should ensure that she complies with this by, for example, advising the client that there are opportunities that the client could undertake, even though the member is unwilling to assist, and recommending that the client seeks alternative advice. Any such discussions should be well documented by the member.

4.13   Ultimately it is the client's decision as to what planning is appropriate having received advice and taking into account their own broader commercial objectives and ethical stance. However, the member should ensure that the client is made aware of the risks and rewards of any planning, including that there may be adverse reputational consequences. It is advisable to ensure that the basis for recommended tax planning is clearly identified in documentation.

4.14   Occasionally a client may advise a member that she intends to proceed with a tax planning arrangement without taking full advice from him on the relevant issues or despite the advice the member has given. In such cases the member should warn the client of the potential risks of proceeding without full advice and ensure that the restriction in the scope of the member's advice is recorded in writing.

4.15   Where a client wishes to pursue a claim for a tax advantage which the member feels has no sustainable basis the member should refer to Chapter 5 Irregularities for further guidance.

4.16   If Counsel's opinion is sought on the planning the member should consider including the question as to whether, in Counsel's view, the GAAR could apply to the transaction.

4.17   It should be noted that any legal opinion provided, for example by Counsel, will be based on the assumptions stated in the instructions for the opinion and on execution of the arrangement exactly as stated. HMRC and the courts will not be constrained by these assumptions.

The different roles of a Tax Adviser

4.18   A member may be involved in tax planning arrangements in the following ways:
- Advising on a planning arrangement.
- Introducing another adviser's planning arrangement.
- Providing a second opinion on a third party's planning arrangement.
- Compliance services in relation to a return which includes a planning arrangement.

A member should always make a record of any advice given.

5. Irregularities

Introduction

5.1   For the purposes of this Chapter, the term 'irregularity' is intended to include all errors whether the error is made by the client, the member, HMRC or any other party involved in a client's tax affairs.

5.2   In the course of a member's relationship with the client, the member may become aware of possible irregularities in the client's tax affairs. Unless already aware of the possible irregularities in question, the client should be informed as soon as the member has knowledge of them.

5.3   Where the irregularity has resulted in the client paying too much tax the member should advise the client about making a repayment claim and have regard to any relevant time limits. With the exception of this paragraph, the rest of this Chapter deals solely with situations where sums may be due to HMRC.

5.4   On occasion, it may be apparent that an error made by HMRC has meant that the client has not paid tax actually due or she has been incorrectly repaid tax. Correcting such mistakes may cause expense to a member and thereby to her clients. A member should bear in mind that, in some circumstances, clients or agents may be able to claim for additional professional costs incurred and compensation from HMRC.

5.5   A member must act correctly from the outset. A member should keep sufficient appropriate records of discussions and advice and when dealing with irregularities the member should:
- Give the client appropriate advice;
- If necessary, so long as she continues to act for the client, seek to persuade the client to behave correctly;
- Take care not to appear to be assisting a client to plan or commit any criminal offence or to conceal any offence which has been committed; and
- In appropriate situations, or where in doubt, discuss the client's situation with a colleague or an independent third party.

5.6   Once aware of a possible irregularity, a member must bear in mind the legislation on money laundering and the obligations and duties which this places upon him.

5.7   A member should also consider whether the irregularity could give rise to a circumstance requiring notification to her professional indemnity insurers.

5.8   In any situation where a member has concerns about her own position, she should take specialist legal advice. This might arise, for example, where a client appears to have used the member to assist in the commission of a criminal offence in such a way that doubt could arise as to whether the member had acted honestly and in good faith.

5.9   The irregularity steps flowchart (5.10) summarises the recommended steps a member should take where a possible irregularity arises.

5.10 Steps to take if there is a possible irregularity

6. Access to data by HMRC

Introduction

6.1   For the purposes of this Chapter the term 'data' includes documents in whatever form (including electronic) and other information. While this guidance relates to HMRC requests, other government bodies or organisations may also approach the member for data. The same principles apply.

6.2   A distinction must be drawn between a request for data made informally and those requests for data which are made in exercise of a power to require the provision of the data requested ('statutory requests').

6.3   Similarly, requests addressed to a client and those addressed to a member require different handling.

6.4   Where a member no longer acts for a client, the member remains subject to the duty of confidentiality.

6.5   A member should comply with reasonable statutory requests and should not seek to frustrate legitimate requests for information. Adopting a constructive approach may help to resolve issues promptly and minimise costs to all parties.

6.6   Whilst a member should be aware of HMRC's powers in relation to the access, inspection and removal of data, given the complexity of the law relating to information powers, it may be appropriate to take specialist advice.

6.7   Revenue Scotland will have separate powers under the Revenue Scotland and Tax Powers Act 2014.

Informal requests addressed to the member

6.8   Disclosure in response to informal requests not made under any statutory power to demand data can only be made with the client's permission.

6.9   Sometimes the client will have authorised routine disclosure of relevant data, for example, through the engagement letter. However, if there is any doubt about whether the client has authorised disclosure or about the accuracy of details, the member should ask the client to approve what is to be disclosed.

6.10   Where an oral enquiry is made by HMRC, a member should consider asking for it to be put in writing so that a response may be agreed with the client.

6.11   Although there is no obligation to comply with an informal request in whole or in part, a member should advise the client whether it is in the client's best interests to disclose such data.

6.12   Informal requests may be forerunners to statutory requests compelling the disclosure of data. Consequently, it may be sensible to comply with such requests or to seek to persuade HMRC that a more limited request is appropriate. The member should advise the client as to the reasonableness of the informal request and likely consequences of not providing the data, so that the client can decide on her preferred course of action.

Informal requests addressed to the client

6.13   From time to time HMRC chooses to communicate directly with clients rather than with the appointed agent.

6.14   HMRC recognises the significant value which tax agents bring to both their clients and to the operation of the tax system. However, HMRC has also made it clear that on occasions it may deal with the taxpayer as well as, or instead of, the agent.

6.15   Examples of where HMRC may contact a member's client directly include:
   • where HMRC is using 'nudge' techniques to encourage taxpayers or claimants to re-check their financial records or to change behaviour;
   • where HMRC has become aware of particular assets, such as offshore investments, and the taxpayer is encouraged to consider whether a further tax disclosure is required;
   • where the taxpayer has engaged in what HMRC considers to be a tax avoidance scheme, as HMRC considers that this will better ensure that the client fully understands HMRC's view.

6.16   HMRC has given reassurances that it is working to ensure that initial contact on compliance checks will normally be via the agent and only if the agent does not reply within an appropriate timescale will the contact be direct to the client.

6.17   When the member assists a client in dealing with such requests from HMRC, the member should apply the principles in 6.8 – 6.12.

Statutory requests addressed to the client

6.18   In advising the client a member should consider whether the notice is valid, how to comply with the request and the consequences of non-compliance. Specialist advice may be needed, for example on such issues as whether the notice has been issued in accordance with the relevant tax legislation, whether the data requested is validly included in the notice, legal professional privilege and human rights.

6.19   Even if the notice is not valid, in many cases the client may conclude that the practical answer is to comply. If the notice is legally effective the client is legally obliged to comply with the request.

6.20   The member should also advise the client about any relevant right of appeal against the statutory request if appropriate and of the consequences of a failure to comply.

Statutory requests addressed to the member

6.21   The same principles apply to statutory requests to the member as statutory requests to clients.

6.22   If a statutory request is valid it overrides the member's duty of confidentiality to her client.

6.23   In cases where the member is not legally precluded by the terms of the notice from communicating with the client, the member should advise the client of the notice and keep the client informed of progress and developments.

6.24   The member remains under a duty to preserve the confidentiality of her client, so care must be taken to ensure that in complying with any notice the member does not provide information or data outside the scope of the notice.

6.25   If a member is faced with a situation in which HMRC is seeking to enforce disclosure by the removal of data, the member should consider seeking immediate advice from a specialist adviser or other practitioner with relevant specialist knowledge, before permitting such removal, to ensure that this is the legally correct course of action.

6.26   Where a Schedule 36 notice is in point a member should note that it does not allow HMRC to inspect business premises occupied by a member in her capacity as an adviser. Specialist advice should be sought in any situation where HMRC asserts otherwise.

Privileged data

6.27   Legal privilege arises under common law and may only be overridden if this is expressly or necessarily implicitly set out in legislation. It protects a party's right to communicate in confidence with a legal adviser. The privilege belongs to the client and not to the member. If a document is privileged:
- The client cannot be required to make disclosure of that document to HMRC and a member should be careful to ensure that her reasons for advising a client nevertheless to make such a disclosure are recorded in writing.
- It must not be disclosed by any other party, including the member, without the client's express permission.

6.28   There are two types of legal privilege under common law, legal advice privilege covering documents passing between a client and her legal adviser prepared for the purposes of obtaining or giving legal advice and litigation privilege for data created for the dominant purpose of litigation. Litigation privilege may arise where litigation has not begun, but is merely contemplated and may apply to data prepared by non-lawyer advisers (including tax advisers) if brought into existence for the purposes of the litigation.

6.29   Communications from a tax adviser who is not a practising lawyer will not attract legal advice privilege but other similar protections exist under statute law, including:
- a privilege reporting exemption which applies to the reporting of money laundering in certain circumstances.
- a privilege under Schedule 36 whereby a tax adviser does not have to provide data that is her property and which constitute communications between the adviser and either her client or another tax adviser of the client. Information about such communications is similarly privileged. However, care should be taken as not all data may be privileged.

6.30   Whether data is or is not privileged and protected from the need to disclose is a complex issue, which will turn on the facts of the particular situation.

6.31   A member who receives a request for data, some of which she believes may be subject to privilege, should take independent legal advice on the position, unless expert in this area.

Reference Material

for AAT Assessment of Personal Tax

Finance Act 2016

Taxation tables for tasks 2-13

For assessments from 1 January – 31 December 2017

Note: this reference material is accessible by candidates during their live computer based assessment for Personal Tax.

Reference material for AAT assessment of Personal Tax

Introduction
This document comprises data that you may need to consult during your Personal Tax computer-based assessment. The material can be consulted during the sample and live assessments through pop-up windows. It is made available here so you can familiarise yourself with the content before the test.

Do not take a print of this document into the exam room with you. Unless you need a printed version as part of reasonable adjustments for particular needs, in which case you must discuss this with your tutor at least six weeks before the assessment date.

This document may be changed to reflect periodical updates in the computer-based assessment, so please check you have the most recent version while studying. This version is based on Finance Act 2016 and is for use in AAT assessments 1 January – 31 December 2017.

Contents

Tax rates and bands

Rates	Bands	Normal rates (%)	Dividend rates (%)
Basic rate	£ 1 - £32,000	20	7.5
Higher rate	£32,001 - £150,000	40	32.5
Additional rate	£150,001 and over	45	38.1

Personal allowances

	£
Personal allowance	11,000
Savings allowance:	
• Basic rate taxpayer	1,000
• Higher rate taxpayer	500
Dividend allowance	5,000
Income limit for personal allowances	100,000

Individual savings accounts

	£
Annual limit	15,240

Car benefit percentage

	%
Emission for petrol engines:	
• 0g/km to 50g/km	7
• 51g/km to 75 g/km	11
• 76g/km to 94g/km	15
• 95g/km or more	16 + 1% for every extra 5g/km above 95g/km
Diesel engines	Additional 3%
Electric vehicles	7%

Car fuel benefit

	£
Base figure	22,200

Approved mileage allowance payments

Mileage	Payment
First 10,000 miles	45p per mile
Over 10,000 miles	25p per mile
Additional passengers (per passenger)	5p per mile
Motorcycles	24p per mile
Bicycles	20p per mile

Van scale charge

	£
Basic charge	3,170
Private fuel charge	598

	%
Benefit charge for zero emission vans	20

Non-taxable benefits

Staff party or event	£150 per head
Incidental overnight expenses:	
• Within the UK	£5 per night
• Overseas	£10 per night
Removal and relocation expenses	£8,000
Non-cash gifts from someone other than the employer	£250 per tax year
Staff suggestion scheme	Up to £5,000
Non-cash long service award	£50 per year of service
Work-related training courses	£15,480 per academic year
Health screening	1 per year
Mobile telephones	1 per employee
Childcare provision:	
• Basic rate taxpayer	£55 per week
• Higher rate taxpayer	£28 per week
• Additional rate taxpayer	£25 per week
Low-rate or interest free loans	Up to £10,000
Subsidised meals	£Nil
Provision of parking spaces	£Nil
Provision of workplace childcare	£Nil
Provision of workplace sports facilities	£Nil
Provision of eye tests and spectacles for VDU use	£Nil
Job-related accommodation	£Nil
Expensive accommodation limit	£75,000
Loan of assets annual charge	20%

HMRC official rate

HMRC official rate	3%

National Insurance contributions

	%
Class 1 Employee:	
• £1 to £8,060	0
• £8,061 to £43,000	12
• £43,001 and above	2
Class 1 Employer:	
• £1 to £8,112	0
• £8,113 and above	13.8
Class 1A	13.8

	£
Employment allowance	3,000

Capital gains tax and tax rates

Capital gains tax	£
Annual exempt amount	11,100
Tax rates	**%**
Basic rate	10
Higher rate	20

Inheritance tax – tax rates

	%
£1 to £325,000	0
Excess:	
• Death rate	40
• Lifetime rate	20

Inheritance tax – taper relief

	% reduction
3 years or less	0
Over 3 years but less than 4 years	20
Over 4 years but less than 5 years	40
Over 5 years but less than 6 years	60
Over 6 years but less than 7 years	80

Inheritance tax – exemptions

	£
Small gifts	250 per transferee per tax year
Marriage or civil partnership:	
• From parent	5,000
• From grandparent	2,500
• From one party to the other	2,500
• From others	1,000
Annual exemption	3,000

Index

for your notes

for your notes

for your notes